David,
Congrats on a great year! I am impressed by your positive attitude, your desire to bring good things to your community, and your dedication to patients looking forward to the years ahead!

—Rebecca

Dr. David Lee

W9-BXY-978

David, I have really enjoyed our conversations that span clinical medicine, doctoring, and metaphysics. You are a deep thinker and empathic individual. Congratulations on completing this chapter and excited to see you in a teacher/manager role

Priyank,

Dear David,
Congratulations on completing intern year! What a milestone! Excited to see where the next few years of training take you.

Best, Rachel Stark

Dear David — I've enjoyed witnessing your compassion & dedication this year. Can't wait to see you continue to develop into your role as a clinician (and @ Windsor!)

Con Cariño, James Lang

Cover design: Flatiron Industries
Text design and composition: Michael E. Ripca
Printed in the United States of America
Printing/Binding: RR Donnelley

**Library of Congress Cataloging-in-Publication Data**

In whatever houses we may visit : an anthology of poems that have inspired physicians / Michael A.
LaCombe, Thomas V. Hartman, editors.
  p. cm.
  Includes bibliographical references.
  ISBN 978-1-934465-06-6
  1. Medicine—Poetry. 2. Physicians—Poetry. 3. Patients—Poetry.
  I. LaCombe, Michael A., 1942–  II. Hartman, Thomas, V., 1966–.
  PN6110.M3I6 2008
  808.81'93561—dc22
                    2008005168

08 09 10 11 12 / 10 9 8 7 6 5 4 3 2 1

*For Physicians everywhere,
and especially
For those in the trenches*

We dance round in a ring and suppose,
But the Secret sits in the middle and knows.

*Robert Frost*

## Medical Litany

From inability to let well alone;
from too much zeal for the new and contempt for what is old;
from putting knowledge before wisdom, science before art, and
cleverness before common sense;
from treating patients as cases;
and from making the cure of the disease more grievous than the
endurance of the same, Good Lord, deliver us.

*Sir Robert Hutchison, MD, MRCP*

# Acknowledgements

Poetry has always been a hard sell in the United States, yet the *Annals of Internal Medicine* has published poetry for over twenty years in its "Ad Libitum" section. For that commitment, we thank those who have served as *Annals* editors: Ed Huth, Bob and Suzanne Fletcher, Frank Davidoff, Christine Laine, and Hal Sox. Moreover, throughout 2007, *Annals* ran a "Call for Poetry," resulting in a huge response from its readership. The following persons, from every corner of the world, sent in their favorite poems for inclusion in this volume:

Pat Onion, Molly Cooke, Martin Donohoe, Johanna Shapiro, Delise Wear, John Burnside, John Bass, Audrey Shafer, David Elpern, Marcia Childress, JoAnn O'Reilly, Robert Farnsworth, Eric Mukai, Richard Berlin, Jose Gros-Aymerich (Madrid), Marc Straus, Richard Thomson, Susan Reese, Peter Richardson, Sarah O'Connor (Scotland), Christine Casey, Elke Galle (Belgium), Felicity Reynolds (London), Peter Raich, Muhammad Ali Syed, Graham Sutton (Leeds, England), Daniel Lewis, Ian Thompson (South Thames, England), Daniel Worthley (Australia), Sally Bastiman (Yarm-North, England), Deborah Swiderski, John Hillery (Ireland), Christopher Woods (Lancashire, England), Miriam Kennedy (Ireland), Gavin Falk (UK), Ian Holdaway (Auckland), Richard Kahn, Michael Alms, Claudia McClintock, Roger Renfrew, N. Mumoli (Italy), Dave Lounsbury, Nicolas Abourizk, Marshall Lichtman, Susan Krantz, James Manning, Reuven Sobel, Clare Cathcart (England), George Lawrence Allen (Edinburgh), Martin Finkel, Gerry Schechter, John Hoesing, Catherine Rees, Marjorie Sirridge, Kevin Kaufhold, Joshua Grossman, Ehab Kasasbeh, Frank Neelon, Mary Brandt, Arthur Chernoff, Stephen Howlett, Kevin Walsh, Kevin Martin, Dewayne Andrews, Stephen Hilty, David Sears, Sachin Goel, Ken Hoekstra, Faith Fitzgerald, John McClenahan, Jeremy Baron (London), David Fisher, Patricia Horne (Dublin), Richard Sobel, Allan Prochazka, Michael Baum, Martin Duke, Stan Deresinski, Howard Holtz, Mark Siegel, Tom Inui, Robin Glassman, Subramanian Somasundaram (Chennai, India), Dena Rifkin, David Nelson, Glenn Cloquhoun (New Zealand), Daniel Mattox, Herbert Keating, George Allen (Edinburgh), Jeremy Smith, Buddha Basnyat (Nepal), David Mast, Cem Sungur (Ankara), and Shah Abdul Latif (Bangladesh).

The editors thank Angela Gabella, Robin Glassman, and Margaret Mary LaCombe for their hard work in making this anthology possible. We acknowledge our debt to the Publications Committee of the American College of Physicians for its vision and support. Finally, we extend our gratitude to the staff of the University of Pennsylvania's Van Pelt Library for their kind assistance throughout the researching of *In Whatever Houses We May Visit*.

# Contents

## Leaning Together in a Storm

## Confronting the Mystery

## So Big a Thing

## Mad Farmers and Homeopathic Blues

# Introduction

The aim of poetry is to give meaning to life. It should explain, define, distill, and focus in ways useful to the reader. Poetry should not be "art for art's sake" – at least, not the kind of poetry we find useful in medicine. Not the sort of poetry found in this anthology. We need to apprehend the moment, express those "thoughts too deep for words," and poetry can get us there. Someone once said that physicians have a front row seat at the drama of life. At such moments one can find no better theater companion than the poet.

Yet, for most physicians, we have found, poetry too often has an overwhelmingly soporific effect, much like a histology lecture at four in the afternoon. This is too often the fault of the poem, not the reader. *Say the words,* is the message, both to poet and to student. Why *jactation,* when *restlessness* will do? Why the obscure reference to Greek mythology, why the arcane word, if not merely to display one's cleverness?

You will find no obscurities in this volume. In every instance, its poems are immediately accessible. They have direct meaning. They give us, many of them, courage, which Garrison Keillor has stated is the purpose of poetry. Here is a test. Turn to John Fallon's "Dissecting Room." If you don't thrill to this one, God help you. Next go to Stafford's "How to Regain Your Soul." Test over. If those poems have moved you, this is a book you must own.

What is remarkable – but really should not have been – is that physicians sent both of those poems to us. As with all the poems sent in, the accompanying notes read something like this:

"Here is *the* poem I keep under my blotter . . . for those hard moments . . . for that encounter . . . when the going gets tough . . . "

In fact, the majority of these poems were sent to us by physicians from all over the world in response to "Call for Poetry" notices sent to virtually every medical journal published in English and a few that are not. A doctor from Ankara sent us a poem by Hikmet, whose "On Living" is pure gold. John Bass, from the literate South and the most literate Southerner we know, suggested a poem by former Poet Laureate Billy Collins. And a country internist provided the Frost couplet at the front of the book. For him, it conveyed the moment of diagnosis, but it distills the profound effect of poetry as well.

There are old warhorses here, such as Donne's "Death Be Not Proud" and Tennyson's "Ulysses," and we debated whether to include them, knowing that both can be found in any comprehensive poetry anthology. Both poems, however, were submitted by a number of physicians. They are great poems because they enlarge our understanding.

*In Whatever Houses We May Visit* is intended for the office desk or for leaning next to Cecil on the shelf in the inner office. We want this book to be more than a gift to doctors, patients, and lovers of poetry. We want it to be *the* anthology containing the reader's favorite poem. Which particular poem, or even what particular subject matter, will of course vary with personal taste. One oncologist, who sent us three poems on death and dying, told us he turns most often to those themes. A geriatrician sent us some priceless poems on aging (among them Sexton's "Courage"). More than one physician saw his or her rural patients in "Soybeans" or in "One Jar, Two Sticks." Not every suggested poem is included here, but many of them had several recommendations.

Mostly these selections are by the icons of poetry such as Yeats, Auden, Sexton, and Sarton, by established modern poets, and by new and emerging poets such as Bosch, Delanty, and Dove. Two poems, however, have been written by "amateurs" who have nevertheless written gems that can hold their own in any anthology: see Masson's "Pathology Report" and Young's "Tell Me."

When it is late at night, when I have been called back to the intensive care unit, when many nurses are working as one over some poor soul found in a ditch, some mother's son — when I watch these nurses, stained and messed with the contamination of disease, frantic with purpose, it is then that I say under my breath:

> *Now tell me again*
> *why you don't believe in angels.*

That is what poetry is for. That is what this anthology is for.

*Michael A. LaCombe, MD*

# Toward Wisdom

## Knowledge and Wisdom

Knowledge and wisdom, far from being one,
Have oftimes no connexion. Knowledge dwells
In heads replete with thoughts of other men;
Wisdom in minds attentive to their own.
Knowledge, a rude unprofitable mass,
The mere material with which Wisdom builds,
Till smoothed and squared, and fitted to its place,
Does but encumber what it means to enrich.
Knowledge is proud that he has learned so much;
Wisdom is humble that he knows no more.

*William Cowper*

## In the Microscope

Here too are dreaming landscapes,
lunar, derelict.
Here too are the masses
tillers of the soil.
And cells, fighters
who lay down their lives
for a song.

Here too are cemeteries,
fame and snow.
And I hear murmuring,
the revolt of immense estates.

*Miroslav Holub*

## Pandora

September.
Second-year medical student.
An early patient interview
at the Massachusetts General Hospital
Routine hernia repair planned, not done.
Abdomen opened and closed.
Filled with disease, cancer.

The patient is fifty-six,
a workingman, Irish
I sit with him, notice
the St. Christopher medal
around his neck.
Can't hurt, can it? he laughs.
I have become his friend.

I bring him a coloring book picture
that shows this thing, this unfamiliar
organ that melted beneath our hands
at dissection:
Pancreas.

Leaving his room, crying,
avoiding classmates,
I take the back stairs.
I find myself locked,
coatless in the courtyard outside.

*Kelley Jean White*

## On Prayer

You ask me how to pray to someone who is not.
All I know is that prayer constructs a velvet bridge
And walking it we are left aloft, as on a springboard
Above landscapes the color of ripe gold
Transformed by a magic stopping of the sun
That velvet bridge leads to the shore of Reversal
Where everything is just the opposite and the word 'is'
Unveils a meaning we hardly envisioned.
Notice: I say we: there, every one, separately,
Feels compassion for others entangled in the flesh
And knows that if there is no other shore
We will walk that aerial bridge all the same.

*Czeslaw Milosz*

## What the Uneducated Old Woman Told Me

That she was glad to sit down.
That her legs hurt in spite of the medicine.
That times were bad.
That her husband had died nearly thirty years before.
That the war had changed things.
That the new priest looked like a schoolboy and you could
    barely hear him in church.
That pigs were better company, generally speaking, than goats.
That no one could fool her.
That both her sons had married stupid women.
That her son-in-law drove a truck.
That he had once delivered something to the President's palace.
That his flat was on the seventh floor and that it made her dizzy
    to think of it.
That he brought her presents from the black market.
That an alarm clock was of no use to her.
That she could no longer walk to town and back.
That all her friends were dead.
That I should be careful about mushrooms.
That ghosts never came to a house where a sprig of rosemary had
    been hung.
That the cinema was a ridiculous invention.
That the modern dances were no good.
That her husband had had a beautiful singing voice, until drink
    ruined it.
That the war had changed things.
That she had seen on a map where the war had been fought.
That Hitler was definitely in Hell right now.
That children were cheekier than ever.
That it was going to be a cold winter, you could tell from the
    height of the birds' nests.
That even salt was expensive these days.
That she had had a long life and was not afraid of dying.
That times were very bad.

*Christopher Reid*

## Earl

In Sitka, because they are fond of them,
People have named the seals. Every seal
is named Earl because they are killed one
after another by the orca, the killer
whale; seal bodies tossed left and right
into the air. "At least he didn't get
Earl," someone says. And sure enough,
after a time, that same friendly,
bewhiskered face bobs to the surface.
It's Earl again. Well, how else are you
to live except by denial, by some
palatable fiction, some little song to
sing while the inevitable, the black and
white blindsiding fact, comes hurtling
toward you out of the deep?

*Louis Jenkins*

# Connoisseur of Chaos

### I

A. A violent order is a disorder; and
B. A great disorder is an order. These
Two things are one. (Pages of illustrations.)

### II

If all the green of spring was blue, and it is;
If all the flowers of South Africa were bright
On the tables of Connecticut, and they are;
If Englishmen lived without tea in Ceylon,
        and they do;
And if it all went on in an orderly way,
And it does; a law of inherent opposites,
Of essential unity, is as pleasant as port,
As pleasant as the brush-strokes of a bough,
An upper, particular bough in, say, Marchand.

### III

After all the pretty contrast of life and death
Proves that these opposite things partake of one,
At least that was the theory, when bishops' books
Resolved the world. We cannot go back to that.
The squirming facts exceed the squamous mind,
If one may say so. And yet relation appears,
A small relation expanding like the shade
Of a cloud on sand, a shape on the side of a hill.

### IV

A. Well, an old order is a violent one.
This proves nothing. Just one more truth, one more
Element in the immense disorder of truths.
B. It is April as I write. The wind
Is blowing after days of constant rain.
All this, of course, will come to summer soon.
But suppose the disorder of truths should ever come
To an order, most Plantagenet, most fixed....

A great disorder is an order. Now, A
And B are not like statuary, posed
For a vista in the Louvre. They are things chalked
On the sidewalk so that the pensive man may see.

V

The pensive man... He sees the eagle float
For which the intricate Alps are a single nest.

*Wallace Stevens*

## Wild Geese

You do not have to be good.
You do not have to walk on your knees
for a hundred miles through the desert, repenting.
You only have to let the soft animal of your body
     love what it loves.
Tell me about despair, yours, and I will tell you mine.
Meanwhile the world goes on.
Meanwhile the sun and the clear pebbles of rain
are moving across the landscapes,
over the prairies and the deep trees,
the mountains and the rivers.
Meanwhile, the wild geese, high in the clean blue air,
are heading home again.
Whoever you are, no matter how lonely,
the world offers itself to your imagination,
calls to you like the wild geese, harsh and exciting—
over and over announcing your place
in the family of things.

*Mary Oliver*

## Lost

Stand still. The trees ahead and bushes beside you
Are not lost. Wherever you are is called Here,
And you must treat it as a powerful stranger,
Must ask permission to know it and be known.
The forest breathes. Listen. It answers,
I have made this place around you.
If you leave it, you may come back again, saying Here.
No two trees are the same to Raven.
No two branches are the same to Wren.
If what a tree or a bush does is lost on you,
You are surely lost. Stand still. The forest knows
Where you are. You must let it find you.

*David Wagoner*

## *From* **The Continuous Life**

What of the neighborhood homes awash
In a silver light, of children crouched in the bushes,
Watching the grown-ups for signs of surrender,
Signs that the irregular pleasures of moving
From day to day, of being adrift on the swell of duty,
Have run their course? Oh parents, confess
To your little ones the night is a long way off
And your taste for the mundane grows; tell them
Your worship of household chores has barely begun;
Describe the beauty of shovels and rakes, brooms and mops;
Say there will always be cooking and cleaning to do,
That one thing leads to another, which leads to another;
Explain that you live between two great darks, the first
With an ending, the second without one, that the luckiest
Thing is having been born, that you live in a blur
Of hours and days, months and years, and believe
It has meaning, despite the occasional fear
You are slipping away with nothing completed, nothing
To prove you existed. Tell the children to come inside,
That your search goes on for something you lost—a name,
A family album that fell from its own small matter
Into another, a piece of the dark that might have been yours,
You don't really know. Say that each of you tries
To keep busy, learning to lean down close and hear
The careless breathing of earth and feel its available
Languor come over you, wave after wave, sending
Small tremors of love through your brief,
Undeniable selves, into your days, and beyond.

*Mark Strand*

## Monet Refuses the Operation

Doctor, you say that there are no haloes
around the streetlights in Paris
and what I see is an aberration
caused by old age, an affliction.
I tell you it has taken me all my life
to arrive at the vision of gas lamps as angels,
to soften and blur and finally banish
the edges you regret I don't see,
to learn that the line I called the horizon
does not exist and sky and water,
so long apart, are the same state of being.
Fifty-four years before I could see
Rouen cathedral is built
of parallel shafts of sun,
and now you want to restore
my youthful errors: fixed
notions of top and bottom,
the illusion of three-dimensional space,
wisteria separate
from the bridge it covers.
What can I say to convince you
the Houses of Parliament dissolve
night after night to become
the fluid dream of the Thames?
I will not return to a universe
of objects that don't know each other,
as if islands were not the lost children
of one great continent. The world
is flux, and light becomes what it touches,
becomes water, lilies on water,
above and below water,
becomes lilac and mauve and yellow
and white and cerulean lamps,
small fists passing sunlight
so quickly to one another
that it would take long, streaming hair
inside my brush to catch it.

To paint the speed of light!
Our weighted shapes, these verticals,
burn to mix with air
and changes our bones, skin, clothes
to gases. Doctor,
if only you could see
how heaven pulls earth into its arms
and how infinitely the heart expands
to claim this world, blue vapor without end.

*Lisel Mueller*

## Nature and Man

Day after day
In vain we labor—
And grow old.

So come,
Empty a cup of wine
With me.

Waste no pity
On the falling blossoms.
Year after year
They will come again
With Spring.

*Wang Wei*

(Translated by Henry Hersch Hart)

## *From* Ode: Intimations of Immortality from Recollections of Early Childhood

…Our birth is but a sleep and a forgetting:
The Soul that rises with us, our life's Star,
　　Hath had elsewhere its setting,
　　　And cometh from afar:
　　Not in entire forgetfulness,
　　And not in utter nakedness,
But trailing clouds of glory do we come
　　From God, who is our home:

…Though nothing can bring back the hour
Of splendour in the grass, of glory in the flower;
　　We will grieve not, rather find
　　Strength in what remains behind;
　　In the primal sympathy
　　Which having been must ever be;
　　In the soothing thoughts that spring
　　Out of human suffering;
　　In the faith that looks through death,
In years that bring the philosophic mind.

…Thanks to the human heart by which we live,
Thanks to its tenderness, its joys, and fears,
To me the meanest flower that blows can give
Thoughts that do often lie too deep for tears.

*William Wordsworth*

## The Makers

Who can remember back to the first poets,
The greatest ones, greater even than Orpheus?
No one has remembered that far back
Or now considers, among the artifacts
And bones and cantilevered inference
The past is made of, those first and greatest poets,
So lofty and disdainful of renown
They left us not a name to know them by.

They were the ones that in whatever tongue
Worded the world, that were the first to say
Star, water, stone, that said the visible
And made it bring invisibles to view
In wind and time and change, and in the mind
Itself that minded the hitherto idiot world
And spoke the speechless world and sang the towers
Of the city into the astonished sky.

They were the first great listeners, attuned
To interval, relationship, and scale,
The first to say above, beneath, beyond,
Conjurors with love, death, sleep, with bread and wine,
Who having uttered vanished from the world
Leaving no memory but the marvelous
Magical elements, the breathing shapes
And stops of breath we build our Babels of.

*Howard Nemerov*

## Forgetfulness

The name of the author is the first to go
followed obediently by the title, the plot
the heartbreaking conclusion, the entire novel
which suddenly becomes one you have never read, never even heard of,

as if, one by one, the memories you used to harbor
decided to retire to the southern hemisphere of the brain,
to a little fishing village where there are no phones.

Long ago you kissed the names of the nine Muses goodbye
and watched the quadratic equation pack its bag,
and even now as you memorize the order of the planets,

something else is slipping away, a state flower, perhaps,
the address of an uncle, the capital of Paraguay.

Whatever it is you are struggling to remember
it is not poised on the tip of your tongue,
not even lurking in some obscure corner of your spleen.

It has floated away down a dark mythological river
whose name begins with an L as far as you can recall,
well on your own way to oblivion where you will join those
who have even forgotten how to swim and how to ride a bicycle.

No wonder you rise in the middle of the night
to look up a date of a famous battle in a book on war.
No wonder the moon in the window seems to have drifted
out of a love poem that you used to know by heart.

*Billy Collins*

## Orders For The Day

Hands, hard and veined all over,
Perform your duties well,
For carelessness can smother
Decision's smoking fuse;
The flesh-bound sighing lover,
His clumsy fingers bruise
The spirit's tender cover.

Feet, bear the thin bones over
The stile of innocence,
Skirt hatred's raging river,
The dangerous flooded plain
Where snake and vulture hover,
And, stalking like a crane,
Cross marshland into clover.

Eyes, staring past another
Whose bogey-haunted look
Reveals a foolish mother,
Those barriers circumvent
And charity discover
Among the virulent.
Breath, turn the old blood over.

*Theodore Roethke*

## How to Regain Your Soul

Come down Canyon Creek trail on a summer
    afternoon
that one place where the valley floor opens out.
    You will see
the white butterflies. Because of the way
    shadows
come off those vertical rocks in the west, there
    are
shafts of sunlight hitting the river and a deep
long purple gorge straight ahead. Put down your
    pack.

Above, air sighs the pines. It was this way
when Rome was clanging, when Troy was being
    built,
when campfires lighted caves. The white
    butterflies dance
by the thousands in the still sunshine. Suddenly
    anything
could happen to you. Your soul pulls toward the
    canyon
and then shines back through the white wings to
    be you again.

*William Stafford*

## Everything is Going to Be All Right

How should I not be glad to contemplate

the clouds clearing beyond the dormer windows

and a high tide reflected on the ceiling?

There will be dying, there will be dying,
but there is no need to go into that.

The lines flow from the hand unbidden
and the hidden source is the watchful heart.

The sun rises in spite of everything
and the far cities are beautiful and bright.

I lie here in a riot of sunlight
watching the day break and the clouds flying.

Everything is going to be all right.

*Derek Mahon*

## The Mystery of Pain

Pain — has an Element of Blank —
It cannot recollect
When it began — or if there were
A time when it was not —

It has no Future — but itself —
Its Infinite realms contain
Its Past — enlightened to perceive
New Periods — of Pain

## [Untitled]

The Heart asks Pleasure — first —
And then — Excuse from Pain —
And then — those little Anodynes
That deaden suffering —

And then — to go to sleep —
And then — if it should be
The will of its Inquisitor
The privilege to die —

## [Untitled]

Faith is a fine invention
        For gentlemen who see;
But microscopes are prudent
In an emergency!

*Emily Dickinson*

## Postscript

And some time make the time to drive out west
Into County Clare, along the Flaggy Shore,
In September or October, when the wind
And the light are working off each other
So that the ocean on one side is wild
With foam and glitter, and inland among stones
The surface of a slate-gray lake is lit
By the earthed lightening of a flock of swans,
Their feathers roughed and ruffling, white on white,
Their fully grown headstrong-looking heads
Tucked or cresting or busy underwater.
Useless to think you'll park and capture it
More thoroughly. You are neither here nor there,
A hurry through which known and strange things pass
As big soft buffetings come at the car sideways
And catch the heart off guard and blow it open.

*Seamus Heaney*

## Dissections

Not only have the skin and flesh and parts of the skeleton
of one of the anatomical effigies in the *Musée de l'Homme*
been excised, stripped away, so that you don't look just at,
but through the thing—pink lungs, red kidney and heart,
tangles of yellowish nerves he seems snarled in, like a net;

not only are his eyes without eyelids, and so shallowly
embedded beneath the blade of the brow, that they seem,
with no shadow to modulate them, flung open in pain or fear;
and not only is his gaze so frenziedly focused that he seems to be
receiving everything, even our regard scraping across him as *blare*;

not only that, but looking more closely, I saw he was real,
that he'd been constructed, reconstructed, on an actual skeleton:
the nerves and organs were wire and plaster, but the armature,
the staring skull, the spine and ribs, were varnished, oxidizing bone;
someone was there, his personhood discernible, a self, a soul.

I felt embarrassed, as though I'd intruded on someone's loneliness,
or grief, and then, I don't know why, it came to me to pray,
though I don't pray, I've unlearned how, to whom, or what,
what fiction, what illusion, or, it wouldn't matter, what true thing,
as mostly I've forgotten how to weep . . . Only mostly, though,

sometimes I can sense the tears in there, and sometimes, yes,
they flow, though rarely for a reason I'd have thought—
a cello's voice will catch in mine, a swerve in a poem, and once,
a death, someone I hardly knew, but I found myself sobbing, sobbing,
for everyone I had known who'd died, and some who almost had.

In the next display hall, evolution: half, then quarter creatures,
Australopithecus, Pithecanthropus, Cro-Magnon,
sidle diffidently along their rocky winding path towards us.
Flint and fire, science and song, and all of it coming to this,
this unhealable self in myself who knows what I should know.

*C. K. Williams*

## With a Million Things to Do, The Doctor Muses, Anyway

Hidden in the office are my favorite
books: *An Anthology of Pain, My Pal
The Cyst, The Innocence of Germs.*
I love my rubber gloves, my darling
smock, the needles and the drugs.

Oh, God, the beauty of disease, the huge
wet cloud it leaves, and then the scenery
of death: whole families dismantled
in the field, those souls all rustling
like wheat, the driver of the bus
announcing up ahead there is a stop
to rest and eat and, on the right, a view.

*Ron Koertge*

## When You Are Old

When you are old and gray and full of sleep,
And nodding by the fire, take down this book,
And slowly read, and dream of the soft look
Your eyes had once, and of their shadows deep;

How many loved your moments of glad grace,
And loved your beauty with love false or true,
But one man loved the pilgrim soul in you,
And loved the sorrows of your changing face;

And bending down beside the glowing bars,
Murmur, a little sadly, how Love fled
And paced upon the mountains overhead
And hid his face amid a crowd of stars.

*W. B. Yeats*

## A Spiral Notebook

The bright wire rolls like a porpoise
in and out of the calm blue sea
of the cover, or perhaps like a sleeper
twisting in and out of his dreams,
for it could hold a record of dreams
if you wanted to buy it for that,
though it seems to be meant for
more serious work, with its
college-ruled lines and its cover
that states in emphatic white letters,
5 SUBJECT NOTEBOOK. It seems
a part of growing old is no longer
to have five subjects, each
demanding an equal share of attention,
set apart by brown cardboard dividers,
but instead to stand in a drugstore
and hang on to one subject
a little too long, like this notebook
you weigh in your hands, passing
your fingers over its surfaces
as if it were some kind of wonder.

*Ted Kooser*

if only
I could clean out the inside
of my body
and stuff it with those
green leaves of daffodils!

*Maekawa Samio*

(Translated by Makoto Ueda)

## Late Fragment

And did you get what
you wanted from this life, even so?
I did.
And what did you want?
To call myself beloved, to feel myself
beloved on the earth.

*Raymond Carver*

## Hooking Rugs and Ice-Fishing

He volunteered with a dying patient
expecting to go through the five stages of grief
at the first meeting. Instead
she talked about hooking rugs:

the needle, the thread, the cloth,
the rhythmic movements of the hands.
He tried other matters in conversation —
she talked of hooking rugs.

On the next visit she spoke of the intricacies
and hardships of ice-fishing that her husband
had done before his death. Week after week,
hooking rugs and ice-fishing.

Angered, he said to friends,
"I can't go on with this
hooking rugs
and ice-fishing."

One day as they sat
in the hospital cafeteria,
she going on, he bored and vexed
with hooking rugs and ice-fishing

the room
went silent, air turned
a luminous shade of green, hooking
rugs and ice

fishing stopped. She leaned over and said,
"I could not have done this
without you,"
then on again with hooking rugs

and ice-fishing. Soon after she died. At the funeral
relatives said to him, "Thank you,
all she ever spoke about
was you."

*Parker Towle*

## Ithaka

As you set out for Ithaka
hope your road is a long one,
full of adventure, full of discovery.
Laistrygonians, Cyclops,
angry Poseidon—don't be afraid of them:
you'll never find things like that on your way
as long as you keep your thoughts raised high,
as long as a rare excitement
stirs your spirit and your body.
Laistrygonians, Cyclops,
wild Poseidon—you won't encounter them
unless you bring them along inside your soul,
unless your soul sets them up in front of you.

Hope your road is a long one.
May there be many summer mornings when,
with what pleasure, what joy,
you enter harbors you're seeing for the first time;
may you stop at Phoenician trading stations
to buy fine things,
mother of pearl and coral, amber and ebony.
sensual perfume of every kind—
as many sensual perfumes as you can;
and may you visit many Egyptian cities
to learn and go on learning from their scholars.

Keep Ithaka always in your mind.
Arriving there is what you're destined for.
But don't hurry the journey at all.
Better if it lasts for years,
so you're old by the time you reach the island,
wealthy with all you've gained on the way,
not expecting Ithaka to make you rich.

Ithaka gave you the marvelous journey.
Without her you wouldn't have set out.
She has nothing left to give you now.

And if you find her poor, Ithaka won't have fooled you.
Wise as you will have become, so full of experience,
you'll have understood by then what these Ithakas mean.

*Constantine P. Cavafy*

(translated by Edmund Keeley and Philip Sherrard)

## Ulysses

It little profits that an idle king,
By this still hearth, among these barren crags,
Match'd with an aged wife, I mete and dole
Unequal laws unto a savage race,
That hoard, and sleep, and feed, and know not me.

I cannot rest from travel: I will drink
Life to the lees: all times I have enjoy'd
Greatly, have suffer'd greatly, both with those
That loved me, and alone; on shore, and when
Thro' scudding drifts the rainy Hyades
Vext the dim sea: I am become a name;
For always roaming with a hungry heart
Much have I seen and known; cities of men
And manners, climates, councils, governments,
Myself not least, but honour'd of them all;
And drunk delight of battle with my peers,
Far on the ringing plains of windy Troy.

I am a part of all that I have met;
Yet all experience is an arch wherethro'
Gleams that untravell'd world, whose margin fades
For ever and for ever when I move.
How dull it is to pause, to make an end,
To rust unburnish'd, not to shine in use!
As tho' to breathe were life. Life piled on life
Were all too little, and of one to me
Little remains: but every hour is saved
From that eternal silence, something more,
A bringer of new things; and vile it were
For some three suns to store and hoard myself,
And this gray spirit yearning in desire
To follow knowledge like a sinking star,
Beyond the utmost bound of human thought.

This is my son, mine own Telemachus,
To whom I leave the sceptre and the isle—
Well-loved of me, discerning to fulfil

This labour, by slow prudence to make mild
A rugged people, and thro' soft degrees
Subdue them to the useful and the good.
Most blameless is he, centred in the sphere
Of common duties, decent not to fail
In offices of tenderness, and pay
Meet adoration to my household gods,
When I am gone. He works his work, I mine.

There lies the port; the vessel puffs her sail:
There gloom the dark broad seas. My mariners,
Souls that have toil'd, and wrought, and thought with me—
That ever with a frolic welcome took
The thunder and the sunshine, and opposed
Free hearts, free foreheads—you and I are old;
Old age hath yet his honour and his toil;
Death closes all: but something ere the end,
Some work of noble note, may yet be done,
Not unbecoming men that strove with Gods.
The lights begin to twinkle from the rocks:
The long day wanes: the slow moon climbs: the deep
Moans round with many voices. Come, my friends,
'Tis not too late to seek a newer world.
Push off, and sitting well in order smite
The sounding furrows; for my purpose holds
To sail beyond the sunset, and the baths
Of all the western stars, until I die.
It may be that the gulfs will wash us down:
It may be we shall touch the Happy Isles,
And see the great Achilles, whom we knew.

Tho' much is taken, much abides; and tho
We are not now that strength which in old days
Moved earth and heaven; that which we are, we are;
One equal temper of heroic hearts,
Made weak by time and fate, but strong in will
To strive, to seek, to find, and not to yield

*Alfred, Lord Tennyson*

## Pathology

Here in the Lord's bosom rest
the tongues of beggars,
the lungs of generals,
the eyes of informers,
the skins of martyrs,

in the absolute
of the microscope's lenses.

I leaf through Old Testament slices of liver,
in the white monuments of brain I read
the hieroglyphs
of decay.

Behold, Christians,
Heaven, Hell, and Paradise
in bottles.
And no wailing,
not even a sigh.
Only the dust moans.
Dumb is history
strained
through capillaries.

Equality dumb. Fraternity dumb.

And out of the tricolours of mortal suffering
we day after day
pull
threads of wisdom.

*Miroslav Holub*

## The Swimming Pool

All around the apt. swimming pool
the boys stare at the girls
and the girls look everywhere but the opposite
or down or up. It is
as it was a thousand years ago: the fat
boy has it hardest, he
takes the sneers,
prefers the winter so he can wear
his heavy pants and sweater.
Today, he's here with the others.
Better they are cruel to him in his presence
than out. Of the five here now (three boys,
two girls) one is fat, three cruel,
and one, a girl, wavers to the side,
all the world tearing at her.
As yet she has no breasts
(her friend does) and were it not
for the forlorn fat boy whom she joins
in taunting, she could not bear her terror,
which is the terror
of being him. Does it make her happy
that she has no need, right now, of ingratiation,
of acting fool to salve
her loneliness? She doesn't seem
so happy. She is like
the lower middle class, that fatal group
handed crumbs so they can drop a few
down lower, to the poor, so they won't kill
the rich. All around
the apt. swimming pool
there is what's everywhere: forsakenness
and fear, a disdain for those beneath us
rather than a rage
against the ones above: the exploiters,
the oblivious and unabashedly cruel.

*Thomas Lux*

# The Subalterns

### I

"Poor wanderer," said the leaden sky,
   "I fain would lighten thee,
But there are laws in force on high
   Which say it must not be."

### II

—"I would not freeze thee, shorn one," cried
   The North, "knew I but how
To warm my breath, to slack my stride;
   But I am ruled as thou."

### III

—"To-morrow I attack thee, wight,"
   Said Sickness. "Yet I swear
I bear thy little ark no spite,
   But am bid enter there."

### IV

—"Come hither, Son," I heard Death say;
   "I did not will a grave
Should end thy pilgrimage to-day,
   But I, too, am a slave!"

### V

We smiled upon each other then,
   And life to me had less
Of that fell look it wore ere when
   They owned their passiveness.

*Thomas Hardy*

## Courage

It is in the small things we see it.
The child's first step,
as awesome as an earthquake.
The first time you rode a bike,
wallowing up the sidewalk.
The first spanking when your heart
went on a journey all alone.
When they called you crybaby
or poor or fatty or crazy
and made you into an alien,
you drank their acid
and concealed it.

Later,
if you faced the death of bombs and bullets
you did not do it with a banner,
you did it with only a hat to
cover your heart.
You did not fondle the weakness inside you
though it was there.
Your courage was a small coal
that you kept swallowing.
If your buddy saved you
and died himself in so doing,
then his courage was not courage,
it was love; love as simple as shaving soap.

Later,
if you have endured a great despair,
then you did it alone,
getting a transfusion from the fire,
picking the scabs off your heart,
then wringing it out like a sock.
Next, my kinsman, you powdered your sorrow,
you gave it a back rub
and then you covered it with a blanket
and after it had slept a while
it woke to the wings of the roses
and was transformed.

Later,
when you face old age and its natural conclusion
your courage will still be shown in the little ways,
each spring will be a sword you'll sharpen,
those you love will live in a fever of love,
and you'll bargain with the calendar
and at the last moment
when death opens the back door
you'll put on your carpet slippers
and stride out.

*Anne Sexton*

## Ask Me

Some time when the river is ice ask me
mistakes I have made. Ask me whether
what I have done is my life. Others
have come in their slow way into
my thought, and some have tried to help
or to hurt: ask me what difference
their strongest love or hate has made.

I will listen to what you say.
You and I can turn and look
at the silent river and wait. We know
the current is there, hidden, and there
are comings and goings from miles away
that hold the stillness exactly before us.
What the river says, that is what I say.

*William Stafford*

## The Woodcarver

Khing, the master carver, made a bell stand
Of precious wood. When it was finished,
All who saw it were astounded. They said it must be
The work of spirits.
The Prince of Lu said to the master carver:
"What is your secret?"

Khing replied: "I am only a workman:
I have no secret. There is only this:
When I began to think about the work you commanded
I guarded my spirit, did not expend it
On trifles, that were not to the point.
I fasted in order to set
My heart at rest.
After three days fasting,
I had forgotten gain and success.
After five days
I had forgotten praise or criticism.
After seven days
I had forgotten my body
With all its limbs.

"By this time all thought of your Highness
And of the court had faded away.
All that might distract me from the work
Had vanished.
I was collected in the single thought
Of the bell stand.

"Then I went to the forest
To see the trees in their own natural state.
When the right tree appeared before my eyes,
The bell stand also appeared in it, clearly, beyond doubt.
All I had to do was to put forth my hand
And begin.

"If I had not met this particular tree
There would have been
No bell stand at all.

"What happened?
My own collected thought
Encountered the hidden potential in the wood;
From this live encounter came the work
Which you ascribe to the spirits.

*Thomas Merton*

## Gratitude to Old Teachers

When we stride or stroll across the frozen lake,
We place our feet where they have never been.
We walk upon the unwalked. But we are uneasy.
Who is down there but our old teachers?

Water that once could take no human weight—
We were students then—holds up our feet,
And goes on ahead of us for a mile.
Beneath us the teachers, and around us the stillness.

*Robert Bly*

# Leaning Together in a Storm

## What The Doctor Said

He said it doesn't look good
he said it looks bad in fact real bad
he said I counted thirty-two of them on one lung before
I quit counting them
I said I'm glad I wouldn't want to know
about any more being there than that
he said are you a religious man do you kneel down
in forest groves and let yourself ask for help
when you come to a waterfall
mist blowing against your face and arms
do you stop and ask for understanding at those moments
I said not yet but I intend to start today
he said I'm real sorry he said
I wish I had some other kind of news to give you
I said Amen and he said something else
I didn't catch and not knowing what else to do
and not wanting him to have to repeat it
and me to have to fully digest it
I just looked at him
for a minute and he looked back it was then
I jumped up and shook hands with this man who'd just given me
something no one else on earth had ever given me
I may have even thanked him habit being so strong

*Raymond Carver*

## Talking to the Family

My white coat waits in the corner
like a father.
I will wear it to meet the sister
in her white shoes and organza dress
in the live of winter,

the milkless husband
holding the baby.

I will tell them.

They will put it together
and take it apart.
Their voices will buzz.
The cut ends of their nerves
will curl.

I will take off the coat,
drive home,
and replace the light bulb in the hall.

*John Stone*

## Anatomy

Two nurses wept—
willow slender, one of them,
the other, fuller bodied.
Breasted, both of them,
thighs smooth beneath thin cotton,
hips, buttocks, curved, comely,
womanly—in honest tears,
reminding me the most important
feature of the female body
is the heart.

*George Bascom*

## Dissecting Room

When these were carried down the road no friends went on
  ahead
To open earth;
There was no little cross upon the grave;
There was no grave.
These are unwanted dead.

Here are the madman and the knave,
The infected harlot, killer, wastrel, sot,
The worthless of the world, raked from its midden
To be dismembered in this air of formalin and rot.

I like to think theirs is a privilege, and bidden
As some return for gentleness forgot or kindness hidden.
For here these worthless find at last a worth
And give their studied flesh to lighten death and life and birth.

*John Fallon*

## One Jar, Two Sticks

Your second home visit
fell on the twelfth of November.
You were in
trailer #8, the one
light green, streaked with rust.

I found you
pissed and suspicious,
buried in poverty,
your three kids milling around.
Your hollow eyes sliver-narrow,
you let me into your home.
Your pale lips pressed white
in anger,
your hands slightly fist-curled.

You had teens to provide for.
Cocky teens, desperately hungry.
I asked social worker type questions.
You stared straight ahead. No reply.

Do you have any food?
When is your next paycheck?
Can I help out somehow?

I opened raw wounds,
and peeled back your pride.

You told me to
open your cupboards.
One by one, they swung open.
Your oldest child left the room, crying,
her fist slamming into the wall.

I found one box of cereal
on its side.
Nothing more.

I had sent you to the food bank
three days before.
What had they given you?

*One jar of peanut butter*
*and two sticks of margarine.*

I cleared the scream from my throat
and left, almost slamming your door.

My supervisor listened to me
rage for an hour . . .
*One jar of peanut butter*
*and two sticks of margarine!*
I broke down in tears.
I broke every rule.
I drove to Shop 'n Save
and piled the cart high.

When I returned it was dark.
I hoped your neighbors wouldn't see me.
(Though who am I kidding?)

I brought you the food.

I set several bags on your counter.
Your kids formed a tight circle around me.
I needed to get the hell out.
They were starving . . . I knew!
But I babbled and stumbled,
apologized
and teared up.

I turned and left
without saying good-bye.
I wanted to hold you
but you would have cringed
had I tried.

One jar, two sticks.
Rural Maine and raw hunger.
I had seen it before,
but never like this.
So desperately hungry,
the gaunt truth
could not be hidden.
(God knows you all tried.)

I couldn't reach far
enough to protect you,
nor bring you close enough
to my side

*Jan Bunford*

## Leaning Together in a Storm

Twelve older men in shirt sleeves
sit around the Cancer Center
sipping ice water and making jokes
waiting for the meeting to begin.
"Ever notice how no one parks
in the Cancer Center zone?"
I am one of them tonight
meant to acknowledge
our story within
our private brotherhood.

The counselor rises to welcome us
asks each to state his cancer story:
give his name and dates
the procedure we chose
tell how long he's survived.
And I take real joy
in hearing them speak
sensing their eyes, their bodies
seated beside me here.

Then a door opens
and our leader rises
to introduce the night's speaker
a young surgeon, his slide-tray at his side.
"Greetings, Gentlemen," he grins
snapping on his slides, projecting
our organs onto the wall,
touching them with his pointer
in blunt precision,
warning us again of lymph nodes
cells outside the prostate
that can end our life.
We swallow a hundred nightmares
with smiles and nods.

I interrupt his gay delivery,
"What about orgasm . . . ?"
"Forget orgasm," he grins,
"You don't have a prostate."
Another asks about second opinions,
"Go ahead . . . what can it hurt?" then adds,
"Unfortunately it won't help much either."
I want to escape this torture by words,
but ask instead, "And what about the
radiation seed implants they're doing in Seattle?"
He turns on me like a cop. "We're doing those now.
So it's a question, how big is your ego?"
Some smile at this, others know
how cold the knife is, how his words
cut across our lives, our wish to live
each breath, see morning spread
across our lawn, our grandchildren's faces.
We all have this unspoken need
to pace our life
like a heart beat.

In the end we let it go
trade our feelings for facts
we already know,
"It's a game of numbers,"
he says again, and I wonder
if these others want to drive
this witch doctor from the room
and gather warmth from the fire
we sit around, share our stories
together of going on

*Larry Smith*

## Coronary Care

Nurses thump my pillow,
bring it back to life,
turn down sheets
and pages of notes,

murmur to themselves
like the machines
that graph my rise
and fall in light.

Rubber bracelets
on wrist and ankle,
a cuff round my arm
that inflates and you,

my red balloon,
lighter than life,
ready to ascend
so easily to heaven.

My bruised red apple
in a bony crate,
you are more delicious
than ever now.

Sweet heart,
you were always there.
Such love I took
for granted. Don't go.

*Christopher J. Woods*

## Parkinson's Disease

While spoon-feeding him with one hand
she holds his hand with her other hand,
or rather lets it rest on top of his,
which is permanently clenched shut.
When he turns his head away, she reaches
around and puts in the spoonful blind.
He will not accept the next morsel
until he has completely chewed this one.
His bright squint tells her he finds
the shrimp she just put in delicious.
She strokes his head very slowly, as if
to cheer up each hair sticking up
from its root in his stricken brain.
Standing behind him, she presses
her cheek to his, kisses his jowl,
and his eyes seem to stop seeing
and do nothing but emit light.
Could heaven be a time, after we are dead,
of remembering the knowledge
flesh had from flesh? The flesh
of his face is hard, perhaps
from years spent facing down others
until they fell back, and harder
from years of being himself faced down
and falling back, and harder still
from all the while frowning
and beaming and worrying and shouting
and probably letting go in rages.
His face softens into a kind
of quizzical wince, as if one
of the other animals were working at
getting the knack of the human smile.
When picking up a cookie he uses
both thumbs to grip it
and push it against an index finger
to secure it so that he can lift it.
She takes him to the bathroom,

and when they come out, she is facing him,
walking backwards in front of him
holding his hands, pulling him
when he stops, reminding him to step
when he forgets and starts to pitch forward.
She is leading her old father into the future
as far as they can go, and she is walking
him back into her childhood, where she stood
in bare feet on the toes of his shoes
and they foxtrotted on this same rug.
I watch them closely: she could be teaching him
the last steps that one day she may teach me.
At this moment, he glints and shines,
as if it will be only a small dislocation
for him to pass from this paradise into the next.

*Galway Kinnell*

## The Last Words Of My English Grandmother

There were some dirty plates
and a glass of milk
beside her on a small table
near the rank, disheveled bed—

Wrinkled and nearly blind
she lay and snored
rousing with anger in her tones
to cry for food,

Gimme something to eat—
They're starving me—
I'm all right I won't go
to the hospital. No, no, no

Give me something to eat
Let me take you
to the hospital, I said
and after you are well

you can do as you please.
She smiled, Yes
you do what you please first
then I can do what I please—

Oh, oh, oh! she cried
as the ambulance men lifted
her to the stretcher—
Is this what you call

making me comfortable?
By now her mind was clear—
Oh you think you're smart
you young people,

she said, but I'll tell you
you don't know anything.
Then we started.
On the way

we passed a long row
of elms. She looked at them
awhile out of
the ambulance window and said,

What are all those
fuzzy-looking things out there?
Trees? Well, I'm tired
of them and rolled her head away.

*William Carlos Williams*

## Like Me

Doctor:
When I was two, my doctor
had a large house
on Cortelyou Road. The exam room
smelled like a dead frog
and my temperature was taken
rectally. By age five
I was injected with tetracycline
monthly by Dr. Ryan.
He later died

of lung cancer. Who influenced me
the most, a medical school
interviewer asked. Thirty years later
I still don't know. Today
a sixteen-year-old girl said
she'd like to be
just like me as I pushed
her third course
of chemotherapy.

*Marc J. Straus*

## Case History

'Most Welshmen are worthless,
an inferior breed, doctor.'
He did not know I was Welsh.
Then he praised the architects
of the German death-camps—
did not know I was a Jew.
He called liberals, 'White blacks',
and continued to invent curses.

When I palpated his liver
I felt the soft liver of Goering;
when I lifted my stethoscope
I heard the heartbeats of Himmler;
when I read his encephalograph
I thought, 'Sieg heil, mein Fuhrer.'

In the clinic's dispensary
red berry of black bryony,
cowbane, deadly nightshade, deathcap.
Yet I prescribed for him
as if he were my brother.

Later that night I must have slept
on my arm: momentarily
my right hand lost its cunning.

*Dannie Abse*

## Afraid So

Is it starting to rain?
Did the check bounce?
Are we out of coffee?
Is this going to hurt?
Could you lose your job?
Did the glass break?
Was the baggage misrouted?
Will this go on my record?
Are you missing much money?
Was anyone injured?
Is the traffic heavy?
Do I have to remove my clothes?
Will it leave a scar?
Must you go?
Will this be in the papers?
Is my time up already?
Are we seeing the understudy?
Will it affect my eyesight?
Did all the books burn?
Are you still smoking?
Is the bone broken?
Will I have to put him to sleep?
Was the car totaled?
Am I responsible for these charges?
Are you contagious?
Will we have to wait long?

*Jeanne Marie Beaumont*

## A Litany in Time of Plague

Adieu, farewell, earth's bliss;
This world uncertain is;
Fond are life's lustful joys;
Death proves them all but toys;
None from his darts can fly;
I am sick, I must die.
    Lord, have mercy on us!

Rich men, trust not in wealth,
Gold cannot buy you health;
Physic himself must fade.
All things to end are made,
The plague full swift goes by;
I am sick, I must die.
    Lord, have mercy on us!

Beauty is but a flower
Which wrinkles will devour;
Brightness falls from the air;
Queens have died young and fair;
Dust hath closed Helen's eye.
I am sick, I must die.
    Lord, have mercy on us!

Strength stoops unto the grave,
Worms feed on Hector brave;
Swords may not fight with fate,
Earth still holds open her gate.
"Come, come!" the bells do cry.
I am sick, I must die.
    Lord, have mercy on us!

Wit with his wantonness
Tasteth death's bitterness;
Hell's executioner
Hath no ears for to hear
What vain art can reply.
I am sick, I must die.
    Lord, have mercy on us!

Haste, therefore, each degree,
To welcome destiny;
Heaven is our heritage,
Earth but a player's stage;
Mount we unto the sky.
I am sick, I must die.
   Lord, have mercy on us!

*Thomas Nashe*

## Stanley Long
BARBITURATE INGESTION

Brief encounter
Across the red blanket
Across a short score of years
For me to pronounce you
Officially finished in my thin black script
For some keeper of records
To fastidiously file.

"Can't understand why a handsome kid...,
Barked the driver of ambulances,
Used to the stink of six-day old bodies.

I knew that you had bravely shared
His lack
Of understanding.

And I noted
Before I replaced your red shroud
That you'd neatly combed your hair
While you waited
To go
To sleep.

*K. D. Beernink*

# Breathing

As I walk up the rise into the silence of snow, in the sough of brittle
    snowflakes,
you are breathing shallow breaths in bed.
A paper tissue lies discarded where I dabbed a drip from your nose.

As I sit in another room you are swishing your lips.
You have become the inside of my body. I am gasping for the crackle
and whistle of your chest. My body is your world under a blanket of snow.

The wolf leaves paw prints on it, catching a niff of tussocky breasts,
dipping thighs, flat tummy, tight skin, the mutter of a bony outcrop.
Hills rise and fall with your breathing, its spate and its whisper.

The snow is lisping from the eaves as I listen for the blab of your heart.
You stir to speak. Your chest heaves. Fistfuls of ice slack off and pelt the stones,
sluds of snow stretch and slide under the window.

There is a quiver, a tingle, then icy water stutters after the snow in a stream.
The night before last, you stopped.
There was a gulp, then stillness and listening — for the lick

of the meniscus on a swollen river, for a trickle in the dried-out bed
of a beck, the jostle of fingertips, snapping of feet. You nestled in a heap
under jacket, quilt, hat, light, scarf, shawl, sheet,

you were all twined and tangled up,
your suck held back by a puff, a spanking sea breeze,
then, flat out, pillows concertinaed, released a salty waft, a redolence

while you held one slippered foot under the sinews, stung and docketed
the twisted jumble, face motionless apart from spitting pith,
and I hoicked you up, straightened the pillows in your shadow

and your voice spurted out as I kibbled your lungs in my own chest's thump.
A sky flipped open when you breathed again, like the tilt over Hartside Top.
No birds. No scratchings. Just rustling of clothes and clacking of teeth.

*Josephine Dickinson*

## Murmur

They cut open his chest
and split the ribs, stitched
bits of leg veins
to the outside of his heart,
patched it all together
and stapled him shut,
sent him home.

Now he feels a turbulence
like a bird fluttering inside him.
As if his heart's old house
has a bad door that won't close,
shudders in the wind.

I place the cold, hard coin
of my stethoscope on his bare chest,
touching down on each of the four places,
medical school's rote lessons a thing of habit
as I listen for the *Tennessee…*
*Tennessee…* of a stiffened ventricle,
the *Kentucky…Kentucky…*
of congestive failure.

Systole, diastole… *lub-*
*dub…lub-dub…,*
I count ten healthy beats,
watch him breathe.

Perhaps it was the two hours on bypass,
the six weeks he missed work
for the first time in his life, or
how like an infant he needed others
to help him rise from a chair,
take his first steps around the unit.

I fold away my stethoscope.
He traces the pink zipper of a scar
down the front of his chest,
tells me he's been married to the same woman

almost fifty years, has a son
who sells life insurance,
a daughter in Topeka, three grandkids.

And now I hear it, too.
How his heart that once said...*today*
...*today*...now seems to say
*remember me...remember me...*

*Peter Pereira*

## Destiny

A hard day—let me see—
a colonoscopy that made me sweat, then
rounds and everybody sick, especially
the gentle pastor failing from lymphoma and the
ninety-year-old trying to recover from her
perforated ulcer, a couple of fevers, and
old Fritz—my German prof, my God, forty
years ago—now bewhiskered, demented with
a meningioma and pneumothorax. Then
the kid celebrating end of term, frolicking
on the roof of his fraternity, falling thirty feet,
crushing skull and spine,
flaccid, serenely intubated, pupils fixed and wide,
somehow hanging on four futile hours. And
a mongrel bit off half
a six-year-old's left ear—he yelled like hell
but let us sew it up. And in the midst
of all this tumult, feeling a serious
satisfaction,
I thought, maybe after all
this *is* what I was meant for.

*George Bascom*

## Therapy

*for Philip*

You attribute my recovery
to *nor trip tyline* —
its effect on neurotransmitters,
on the *a myg dala.*

You barely nod towards your worth —
insisting on blood levels,
on a therapeutic dose.

While I credit half our success
to the pear tree blossoming white
beyond your left shoulder,

to the wisteria —
its pink flowers hanging
lush and fragrant
over the portico,

to the warmth of your hand.

*John Wright*

## Open You Up

The smile was fear.
20 pack-years and a few month's cough—
a steelworker from Gary,
X ray lit with a lesion
round and opaque as a silver dollar.
I wanted to tell him,
to pull the curtain around us
and sit beside him on his bed,
to break the news
soft as a surgeon's hand.

But I swaggered and stood
like a half-drunk general:
*You've got something in your chest*
*and we've got to open you up.*
I can't remember his response
just the flame in my cheeks
and our meeting months later,
his face the color of fly ash.
So much bone when he hugged me
like my father before he died,
the emptiness in my chest,
something opened up, forever.

*Richard M. Berlin*

## The Dance

A middle-aged woman, quite plain, to be polite about it, and
   somewhat stout, to be more courteous still,
but when she and the rather good-looking, much younger man she's with
   get up to dance,
her forearm descends with such delicate lightness, such restrained but
   confident ardor athwart his shoulder,
drawing him to her with such a firm, compelling warmth, and moving
   him with effortless grace
into the union she's instantly established with the not at all rhythmically
   solid music in this second-rate café,

that something in the rest of us, some doubt about ourselves, some sad
   conjecture, seems to be allayed,
nothing that we'd ever thought of as a real lack, nothing not to be
   admired or be repentant for,
but something to which we've never adequately given credence,
which might have consoling implications about how we misbelieve
   ourselves, and so the world,
that world beyond us which so often disappoints, but which
   sometimes shows us, lovely, what we are.

*C. K. Williams*

## Having it Out with Melancholy

"If many remedies are prescribed for an illness, you may be certain that the illness has no cure."

A. P. Chekhov, *The Cherry Orchard*

### 1  FROM THE NURSERY

When I was born, you waited
behind a pile of linen in the nursery,
and when we were alone, you lay down
on top of me, pressing
the bile of desolation into every pore.

And from that day on
everything under the sun and moon
made me sad — even the yellow
wooden beads that slid and spun
along a spindle on my crib.

You taught me to exist without gratitude.
You ruined my manners toward God:
"We're here simply to wait for death;
the pleasures of earth are overrated."

I only appeared to belong to my mother,
to live among blocks and cotton undershirts
with snaps; among red tin lunch boxes
and report cards in ugly brown slipcases.
I was already yours — the anti-urge,
the mutilator of souls.

### 2  BOTTLES

Elavil, Ludiomil, Doxepin,
Norpramin, Prozac, Lithium, Xanax,
Wellbutrin, Parnate, Nardil, Zoloft.
The coated ones smell sweet or have
no smell; the powdery ones smell
like the chemistry lab at school
that made me hold my breath.

3  SUGGESTION FROM A FRIEND

You wouldn't be so depressed
if you really believed in God.


4  OFTEN

Often I go to bed as soon after dinner
as seems adult
(I mean I try to wait for dark)
in order to push away
from the massive pain in sleep's
frail wicker coracle.


5  ONCE THERE WAS LIGHT

Once, in my early thirties, I saw
that I was a speck of light in the great
river of light that undulates through time.

I was floating with the whole
human family. We were all colors — those
who are living now, those who have died,
those who are not yet born. For a few

moments I floated, completely calm,
and I no longer hated having to exist.

Like a crow who smells hot blood
you came flying to pull me out
of the glowing stream.
"I'll hold you up. I never let my dear
ones drown!" After that, I wept for days.


6  IN AND OUT

The dog searches until he finds me
upstairs, lies down with a clatter
of elbows, puts his head on my foot.

Sometimes the sound of his breathing
saves my life — in and out, in
and out; a pause, a long sigh....


7  PARDON

A piece of burned meat
wears my clothes, speaks
in my voice, dispatches obligations
haltingly, or not at all.
It is tired of trying
to be stouthearted, tired
beyond measure.

We move on to the monoamine
oxidase inhibitors. Day and night
I feel as if I had drunk six cups
of coffee, but the pain stops
abruptly. With the wonder
and bitterness of someone pardoned
for a crime she did not commit
I come back to marriage and friends,
to pink fringed hollyhocks; come back
to my desk, books, and chair.


8  CREDO

Pharmaceutical wonders are at work
but I believe only in this moment
of well-being. Unholy ghost,
you are certain to come again.

Coarse, mean, you'll put your feet
on the coffee table, lean back,
and turn me into someone who can't
take the trouble to speak; someone
who can't sleep, or who does nothing
but sleep; can't read, or call
for an appointment for help.

There is nothing I can do
against your coming.
*When I awake, I am still with thee.*


9  WOOD THRUSH

High on Nardil and June light
I wake at four,
waiting greedily for the first
note of the wood thrush. Easeful air
presses through the screen
with the wild, complex song
of the bird, and I am overcome

by ordinary contentment.
What hurt me so terribly
all my life until this moment?
How I love the small, swiftly
beating heart of the bird
singing in the great maples;
its bright, unequivocal eye.

*Jane Kenyon*

## Terminal

The eight years difference in age seems now
Disparity so wide between the two
That when I see the man who armoured stood
Resistant to all help however good
Now helped through day itself, eased into chairs,
Or else led step by step down the long stairs
With firm and gentle guidance by his friend,
Who loves him, through each effort to descend,
Each wavering, each attempt made to complete
An arc of movement and bring down the feet
As if with that spare strength he used to enjoy,
I think of Oedipus, old, led by a boy.

*Thom Gunn*

## Soybeans

The October air was warm and musky, blowing
Over brown fields, heavy with the fragrance
Of freshly combined beans, the breath of harvest.

He was pulling a truckload onto the scales
At the elevator near the rail siding north of town
When a big Cadillac drove up. A man stepped out,
Wearing a three-piece suit and a gold pinky ring.
The man said he had just invested a hundred grand
In soybeans and wanted to see what they looked like.

The farmer stared at the man and was quiet, reaching
For the tobacco in the rear pocket of his jeans,
Where he wore *his* only ring, a threadbare circle rubbed
By working cans of dip and long hours on the backside
Of a hundred acre run. He scooped up a handful
Of small white beans, the pearls of the prairie, saying:

Soybeans look like a foot of water on the field in April
When you're ready to plant and can't get in;
Like three kids at the kitchen table
Eating macaroni and cheese five nights in a row;
Or like a broken part on the combine when
Your credit with the implement dealer is nearly tapped.

Soybeans look like prayers bouncing off the ceiling
When prices on the Chicago grain market start to drop;
Or like your old man's tears when you tell him
How much the land might bring for subdivisions.
Soybeans look like the first good night of sleep in weeks
When you unload at the elevator and the kids get Christmas.

He spat a little juice on the tire of the Cadillac,
Laughing despite himself and saying to the man:
Now maybe you can tell me what a hundred grand looks like.

*Thomas Alan Orr*

## Osler

An eye whose magic wakes the hidden springs
Of slumbering fancy in the weary mind.
A tongue that dances with the ready word
That like an arrow, seeks its chosen goal,
And piercing all the barriers of care,
Opens the way to warming rays of hope.
A presence like the freshening breeze that as
It passes, sweeps the poisoned cloud aside.
An ear that 'mid the discords of the day,
Swings to the basic harmonies of life.
A heart whose alchemy transforms the dross
Of dull suspicion to the gold of love.
A spirit like the fragrance of some flower
That lingers round the spot that this has graced,
To tell us that although the rose be plucked
And spread its perfume throughout distant halls,
The vestige of its sweetness quickens still
The conscience of the precinct where it bloomed.

*William Sydney Thayer*

## Death of a Psychiatrist

*For Volta Hall*

1

Now the long lucid listening is done,
Where shame and anguish were subtly opposed:
His patients mourn this father as their own.

Each was accepted whole and wholly known,
Down to the deepest naked need exposed.
Now the long lucid listening is done.

For the raw babe, he was a healing zone.
The cry was heard; the rage was not refused.
Each has a father to mourn as his own.

When someone sees at last, the shame is gone;
When someone hears, anguish may be composed,
And the long lucid listening is done.

The ghostly child goes forth once more alone,
And scars remain, but the deep wound is closed.
Each has a father to mourn as his own.

A guiltless loss, this shines like a sun,
And love remains, but the deep wound is closed.
Each has a father to mourn as his own,
Now the long lucid listening is done.

2

It was not listening alone, but hearing,
For he remembered every crucial word
And gave one back oneself because he heard.

Who listens so, does more than listen well.
He goes down with his patient into Hell.

It was not listening alone, but healing.
We knew a total, yet detached response,
Harsh laugh, sane and ironical at once.

Who listens so, does more than merely pity,
Restores the soul to its lost dignity.

It was not listening alone, but sharing.
And I remember how he bowed his head
Before a poem. "Read it again," he said.

Then, in the richest silence he could give,
I saw the poem born, knew it would live.

It was not listening alone, but being.
We saw a face so deeply lined and taut
It wore the passion of dispassionate thought.

Because he cared, he heard; because he heard,
He lifted, shared, and healed without a word.

*May Sarton*

## Angina Pectoris

If half my heart is here, doctor,
the other half is in China
with the army flowing
toward the Yellow River.
And, every morning, doctor,
every morning at sunrise my heart
is shot in Greece.
And every night, doctor,
when the prisoners are asleep and the infirmary is deserted,
my heart stops at a rundown old house
in Istanbul.
And then after ten years,
all I have to offer my poor people
is this apple in my hand, doctor,
one red apple:
my heart.
And that, doctor, that is the reason
for this angina pectoris –
not nicotine, prison or arteriosclerosis
I look at the night through the bars,
and despite the weight on my chest,
my heart still beats with the most distant stars.

*Nazim Hikmet*

(translated by Mutlu Konuk and Randy Blasing)

## Going Deaf

No matter how she tilts her head to hear
she sees the irritation in their eyes.
She knows how they can read a small rejection,
a little judgment, in every *What did you say?*
So now she doesn't say *What?* or *Come again?*
She lets the syllables settle, hoping they form
some sort of shape that she might recognize.
When they don't, she smiles with everyone else,
and then whoever was talking turns to her
and says, "Break wooden coffee, don't you know?"
She puts all she can focus into the face
to know if she ought to nod or shake her head.
In that long space her brain talks to itself.
The person may turn away as an act of mercy,
leaving her there in a room full of understanding
with nothing to cover her, neither sound nor silence.

*Miller Williams*

# Confronting the Mystery

## To Death

You will come in any case—so why not now?
I am waiting for you—I can't stand much more.
I've put out the light and opened the door
For you, so simple and miraculous.
So come in any form you please,
Burst in as a gas shell
Or, like a gangster, steal in with a length of pipe,
Or poison me with typhus fumes.
Or be that fairy tale you've dreamed up,
So sickeningly familiar to everyone—
In which I glimpse the top of a pale blue cap
And the house attendant white with fear.
Now it doesn't matter anymore. The Yenisey swirls,
The North Star shines.
And the final horror dims
The blue luster of beloved eyes.

*Anna Akhmatova*

(translated by Judith Hemschemeyer)

## For My Mother Ill

I'll join you in your sleep,
into the same darkness dive,
where dead fish float together.
But we shall be communing,
blindly and without feeling,
by knowing now,
as I lay back upon a pillow,
as you close your eyes,
its comfort.

*David Ignatow*

## Funeral Blues

Stop all the clocks, cut off the telephone,
Prevent the dog from barking with a juicy bone,
Silence the pianos and with muffled drum
Bring out the coffin, let the mourners come.

Let aeroplanes circle moaning overhead
Scribbling on the sky the message 'He is Dead'.
Put crepe bows round the white necks of the public doves,
Let the traffic policemen wear black cotton gloves.

He was my North, my South, my East and West,
My working week and my Sunday rest,
My noon, my midnight, my talk, my song;
I thought that love would last forever: I was wrong.

The stars are not wanted now; put out every one,
Pack up the moon and dismantle the sun,
Pour away the ocean and sweep up the woods;
For nothing now can ever come to any good.

*W. H. Auden*

## To an American Poet Just Dead

In the *Boston Sunday Herald* just three lines
Of no-point type for you who used to sing
The praises of imaginary wines,
And died, or so I'm told, of the real thing.

Also gone, but a lot less forgotten,
Are an eminent cut-rate druggist, a lover of Giving,
A lender, and various brokers: gone from this rotten
Taxable world to a higher standard of living.

It is out of the comfy suburbs I read you are dead,
And the soupy summer is settling, full of the yawns
Of Sunday fathers loitering late in bed,
And the ssshh of sprays on all the little lawns.

Will the sprays weep wide for you their chaplet tears?
For you will the deep-freeze units melt and mourn?
For you will Studebakers shred their gears
And sound from each garage a muted horn?

They won't. In summer sunk and stupefied
The suburbs deepen in their sleep of death.
And though they sleep the sounder since you died
It's just as well that now you save your breath.

*Richard Wilbur*

## For a Lost Child

What happens is, the kind of snow that sweeps
Wyoming comes down while I'm asleep. Dawn
finds our sleeping bag but you are gone.
Nowhere now, you call through every storm,
a voice that wanders without a home.

Across bridges that used to find a shore
you pass, and along shadows of trees that fell
before you were born. You are a memory
too strong to leave this world that slips away
even as its precious time goes on.

I glimpse you often, faithful to every country
we ever found, a bright shadow the sun
forgot one day. On a map of Spain
I find your note left from a trip that year
our family traveled: "Daddy, we could meet
   here."

*William Stafford*

## Sonnet XVI

*from* "Sonnets from an Ungrafted Tree"
(*The Harp Weaver and Other Poems*)


The doctor asked her what she wanted done
With him, that could not lie there many days.
And she was shocked to see how life goes on
Even after death, in irritating ways;
And mused how if he had not died at all
'Twould have been easier—then there need not be
The stiff disorder of a funeral
Everywhere, and the hideous industry,
And crowds of people calling her by name
And questioning her, she'd never seen before,
But only watching by his bed once more
And sitting silent if a knocking came...
She said at length, feeling the doctor's eyes,
"I don't know what you do exactly when a person dies."

*Edna St. Vincent Millay*

## *From* **Spring, Summer and Autumn**

Now is Death merciful. He calls me hence
   Gently, with friendly soothing of my fears
   Of ugly age and feeble impotence
   And cruel disintegration of slow years.
   Nor does he leap upon me unaware
   Like some wild beast that hungers for its prey,
   But gives me kindly warning to prepare
   Before I go, to kiss your tears away.

   How sweet the summer! And the autumn shone
   Late warmth within our hearts as in the sky,
   Ripening rich harvests that our love had sown.
   How good that ere the winter comes, I die!
   Then, ageless, in your heart I'll come to rest
   Serene and proud as when you loved me best.

*Hans Zinsser*

## The Shape of Death

What does love look like? We know
the shape of death. Death is a cloud
immense and awesome. At first a lid
is lifted from the eye of light:
there is a clap of sound, a white blossom

belches from the jaw of fright,
a pillared cloud churns from white to gray
like a monstrous brain that bursts and burns,
then turns sickly black, spilling away,
filling the whole sky with ashes of dread;

thickly it wraps, between the clean sea
and the moon, the earth's green head.
Trapped in its cocoon, its choking breath
we know the shape of death:
Death is a cloud.

What does love look like?
Is it a particle, a star -
invisible entirely, beyond the microscope and Palomar?
A dimension unimagined, past the length of hope?
Is it a climate far and fair that we shall never dare

discover? What is its color, and its alchemy?
Is it a jewel in the earth-can it be dug?
Or dredged from the sea? Can it be bought?
Can it be sown and harvested?
Is it a shy beast to be caught?

Death is a cloud,
immense, a clap of sound.
Love is little and not loud.
It nests within each cell, and it
cannot be split.

It is a ray, a seed, a note, a word,
a secret motion of our air and blood.
It is not alien, it is near-
our very skin-
a sheath to keep us pure of fear.

*May Swenson*

## The Race

When I got to the airport I rushed up to the desk
and they told me the flight was cancelled. The doctors had
said my father would not live through the night
and the flight was cancelled. A young man with a
dark blond mustache told me
another airline had a non-stop
leaving in seven minutes — see that
elevator over there well go
down to the first floor, make a right you'll
see a yellow bus, get off at the
second Pan Am terminal — I
ran, I who have no sense of direction
raced exactly where he'd told me, like a fish
slipping upstream deftly against the
flow of the river. I jumped off that bus with my
heavy bags and ran, the bags
wagged me from side to side as if to
prove I was under the claims of material. I
ran up to a man with a white flower on his breast,
I who always go to the end of the line, I said
Help me. He looked at my ticket, he said make a
left and then a right go up the moving stairs and then
run. I raced up the moving stairs
two at a time, at the top I saw the
long hollow corridor and
then I took a deep breath, I said
goodbye to my body, goodbye to comfort, I
used my legs and heart as if I would
gladly use them up for this, to
touch him again in this life. I ran and the
big heavy dark bags
banged me, wheeled and swam around me like
planets in wild orbits — I have seen
pictures of women running down roads with their
belongings tied in black scarves

grasped in their fists, running under serious
gray historical skies —
                I blessed my
long legs he gave me, my strong
heart I abandoned to its own purpose, I
ran to Gate 17 and they were just lifting the thick white
lozenge of the door to fit it into the
socket of the plane, Like the man who is not
too rich, I turned to the side and
slipped trough the needle's eye, and then I
walked down the aisle toward my father. The jet was
full and people's hair was shining, they were
smiling, the interior of the plane was filled with a
mist of gold endorphin light,
I wept as people weep when they enter heaven,
in massive relief. We lifted up
gently from on tip of the continent and
did not stop until we sat down lightly on the
other edge, I walked into his room and
watched his chest rise slowly and
sink again, all night
I watched him breathe.

*Sharon Olds*

## Time Heals All Wounds — But One

He was a huge
hulk of a man
but the blade cut his belly
like it was a melon.
He was cheerful at first
but as weeks wore on
like his cheap shoes
and time spun out
with miles of gauze packing,
his wound stank
and Leroy shrank
shriveled nearly
to skin and skeleton.
One day, barely
conscious, he whispered:
"Let me go, Doc,"
and I did.

*Vernon Rowe*

## Death Benefits

We have a small burial allotment
set aside for cases like this,
and a large American flag
you can pick up at the office
during working hours, or have sent
to your home, but not in time
for the funeral.

There is also a form to fill out
in case he was orphaned, or damaged
when young, or his mind
took a turn for the worse — but only
if the turn occurred in the war —
in which case your loved one
may get something else.

Sometimes survivors ask questions
regarding what happened —
Did my loved one have pain in the end?
Could he have survived, if things
had gone differently? We suggest
you think twice before asking.
These questions won't bring him back.

In summary, we did everything we could.
We did even more than was expected
of us. We worked double shifts, often
without lunch, often half-sick ourselves.
No one has ever cared for a person
the way we cared for your loved one.
Please accept our regrets.

*Jack Coulehan*

# yohaku[1]

*for Richard Katz*

there would be
no rain there, the
empty husks crumbling,
pretending to
be god's voices
would not be some
where else
the night
whose darkness will reveal
nothing is there, but
here also.
I hold my empty hand.
the birds will miss you.

*elmo holder*

[1]Yohaku — the empty white space in Japanese ink drawings.

## Old Folks Laugh

They have spent their
content of simpering,
holding their lips this
and that way, winding
the lines between
their brows. Old folks
allow their bellies to jiggle like slow
tamborines.

*The hollers*
rise up and spill
over any way they want.
When old folks laugh, they free the world.
They turn slowly, slyly knowing
the best and the worst
of remembering.
Saliva glistens in
the corners of their mouths,
their heads wobble
on brittle necks, but
their laps
are filled with memories.
When old folks laugh, they consider the promise
of dear painless death, and generously
forgive life for happening
to them.

*Maya Angelou*

## Death

I have seen   come on
slowly as rust
sand

or suddenly   as when
someone leaving
a room

finds the doorknob
come loose in his hand

*John Stone*

## When Death Comes

When death comes
like the hungry bear in autumn;
when death comes and takes all the bright coins from his purse

to buy me, and snaps the purse shut;
when death comes
like the measles-pox;

when death comes
like an iceberg between the shoulder blades,

I want to step through the door full of curiosity, wondering:
what is it going to be like, that cottage of darkness?

And therefore I look upon everything
as a brotherhood and a sisterhood,
and I look upon time as no more than an idea,
and I consider eternity as another possibility,

and I think of each life as a flower, as common
as a field daisy, and as singular,

and each name a comfortable music in the mouth
tending as all music does, toward silence,

and each body a lion of courage, and something
precious to the earth.

When it's over, I want to say: all my life
I was a bride married to amazement.
I was the bridegroom, taking the world into my arms.

When it is over, I don't want to wonder
if I have made of my life something particular, and real.
I don't want to find myself sighing and frightened,
or full of argument.

I don't want to end up simply having visited this world.

*Mary Oliver*

## Hospital Visits

At length to hospital
This man was limited,
Where screens leant on the wall
And idle headphones hung.
Since he would soon be dead
They let his wife come along
And pour out tea, each day.

I don't know what was said;
Just hospital-talk,
As the bed was a hospital bed.
Then one day she fell
Outside on the sad walk
And her wrist broke — curable
At Outpatients, naturally.

Thereafter night and day
She came both for the sight
Of his slowing-down body
And for her own attending,
And there by day and night
With her blithe bone mending
Watched him in decay.

Winter had nearly ended
When he died (the screen was for that).
To make sure her wrist mended
They had her in again
To finish a raffia mat —
This meant (since it was begun
Weeks back) he died again as she came away.

*Philip Larkin*

## To Florida

Southward floated over
The vicious little houses, down
The land. Past Carolina, where
The bloom began
Beneath their throbbing clouds, they fed us
Coldcuts, free. We had our choice.
Below, the seasons twist; years
Roll backward toward the can
Like film, and the mistake appears,
To scale, soundlessly. The signs
Light up. Across the aisle
An old man twitches in his sleep. His mind
Will firm in time. His health
Will meet him at the terminal.

*Louise Glück*

## Still Life

I shall not soon forget
The greyish-yellow skin
To which the face had set:
Lids tight: nothing of his,
No tremor from within,
Played on the surfaces.

He still found breath, and yet
It was an obscure knack.
I shall not soon forget
The angle of his head,
Arrested and reared back
On the crisp field of bed,

Back from what he could neither
Accept, as one opposed,
Nor, as a life-long breather,
Consentingly let go,
The tube his mouth enclosed
In an astonished O.

*Thom Gunn*

## My Grandfather Dying

I could see bruises or shadows
deep under his skin, like the shapes
skaters find frozen in rivers—
leaves caught in flight,
or maybe the hand of a man reaching up
out of the darkness for help.

I was helpless as flowers
there at his bedside. I watched
his legs jerk in the sheets.
He answered doors,
he kicked loose stones from his fields.
I leaned down to call out my name
and he called it back. His breath
was as sour as an orchard
after the first frost.

*Ted Kooser*

## Obituaries

These are no pages for the young,
who are better off in one another's arms,

nor for those who just need to know
about the price of gold,
or a hurricane that is ripping up the Keys.

But eventually you may join
the crowd who turn here first to see
who has fallen in the night,
who has left a shape of air walking in their place.

Here is where the final cards are shown,
the age, the cause, the plaque of deeds,
and sometimes an odd scrap of news—
that she collected sugar bowls,
that he played solitaire without any clothes.

And all the survivors huddle at the end
under the roof of a paragraph
as if they had sidestepped the flame of death.

What better way to place a thin black frame
around the things of the morning—
the hand-painted cup,
the hemispheres of a cut orange,
the slant of sunlight on the table?

And sometimes a most peculiar pair turns up,
strange roommates lying there
side by side upon the page—
Arthur Godfrey next to Man Ray,
Ken Kesey by the side of Dale Evans.

It is enough to bring to mind an ark of death,
not the couples of the animal kingdom,
but rather pairs of men and women
ascending the gangplank two by two,

surgeon and model,
balloonist and metalworker,
an archeologist and an authority on pain.

Arm in arm, they get on board
then join the others leaning on the rails,
all saved at last from the awful flood of life—

so many of them every day
there would have to be many arks,
an armada to ferry the dead
over the heavy waters that roll beyond the world,

and many Noahs too,
bearded and fiercely browed, vigilant up there at every prow.

*Billy Collins*

## Terminally Ill

Every morning he is astounded again,
always for the first time,
every time more violently than before.

He is astounded relentlessly,
with impressive energy,
passionately, fiercely, vehemently,
till he is out of breath.

He pants with astonishment,
he chokes,
he gluts himself on astonishment,
he drowns like a puppy thrown into deep water,
he shivers, trembles, cries with astonishment.

That the affliction came to him
against which there is no help.

*Anna Swir*

(translated by Czeslaw Milosz with Leonard Nathan)

## Massive Trauma

The tractor tipped, pinned
the powerful young farmer,
crushed his pelvis, tore
unseen arteries and veins
that instantly began to spill
his thundering and waning blood.
We snatched him from a screaming ambulance—
torn and dirt-stained overalls, IV's everywhere—
and bounced him into OR 2
on a frantic, rattling litter.
   As we heaved his pale, loose bulk,
dirt and all, over to the table,
he fibrillated.
Pulses racing, scared, we tried to get him back,
shocked, squeezed his heart,
poured in blood, opened
his belly, packed his bleeders.
Then we waited, having done our job,
joked a little, watched the blood pour in.
   When the EKG went flat, stayed flat,
we sighed and said our thanks, stripped off
our gowns and gloves, pulled off our masks,
and then against the broken
wailing of his wife
walked unprotected down the corridor
to what we had been hiding from.

*George Bascom*

# Departures

They seemed to all take off
at once: Aunt Grace
whose kidneys closed shop;
Cousin Rose who fed sugar
to diabetes;
my grandmother's friend
who postponed going so long
we thought she'd stay.

It was like the summer years ago
when they all set out on trains
and ships, wearing hats with veils
and the proper gloves,
because everybody was going
someplace that year,
and they didn't want
to be left behind.

*Linda Pastan*

Buffalo Bill's

defunct

      who used to

      ride a watersmooth-silver

                 stallion

and break onetwothreefourfive pigeonsjustlikethat

                         Jesus

he was a handsome man

          and what i want to know is

how do you like your blueeyed boy

Mister Death

        *E. E. Cummings*

## A Boat Is a Lever

      —after Simone Weil

After my student went to the doctor to
Check out the rash speckling his
Right hand and found out he had
Leukemia, that the cancer had spread
Into his lungs, then where did he go?
I've called his number several times.
Flat-bottom boats light in water.
Brown brack and mud smell,
Stumps like chewed-off candles,
Cypress knees, knock and small
Talk floating over water, a motor
Chuffing off, a small blue cloud of excess
Gasoline spreads an ugly
Rainbow on tan water.  Every
Thing rests on its proposition
Including smooth isobars along the bay.
*Since collective thought cannot exist*
*As thought it passes into things.*
Chemo takes a few gray hairs. Mustard
Cruises the bloodstream under a blizzard
Of white cells. Subdued by the arbitrary,
Suspended, the one in the boat still needs
To row it — to direct the muscles, to
Maintain equilibrium with air
And water. If water is waveless
Then the boat reads by leading marks.
*There is nothing more beautiful*
*Than a boat.*

                      *Ralph Burns*

## A Man In Maine

North. The bare time.
The same quick dark
from Rutland to Nome,

the utter chill.
Winter stars. After
work, splitting birch

by the light outside
his back door, a man
in Maine thinks what

his father told him,
splitting outside
this same back door:

every November, his
father said, he thought
when he split wood

of what his father
said the night he
right here died: just

after supper, his
father said, his father
came out back, looked

out at the sky
the way he had
for years, picked up

his ax, struck
the oak clean, and
was himself struck

down; before he
died he just had
this to say:

*this time of*
*year the stars*
*come close some fierce.*

*Philip Booth*

## At My Funeral

I take a seat in the third row
and catch the eulogies. It's sweet
to see old friends, some I don't know.
I wear a tie, good shoes, and greet
a stranger with a kiss. It's bliss
for an insecure guy to hear
deep words. I'll live on them, not miss
a throb, and none of us will fear
the night. There are no tears, no sad
faces, no body or sick word
of God. I sing, have a warm chat
with friends gone sour, wipe away bad
blood. And sweet loves? I tell a bird
to tip them off. Then tip my hat.

*Willis Barnstone*

## Death Be Not Proud

Death be not proud, though some have called thee
Mighty and dreadfull, for, thou art not so,
For, those, whom thou think'st, thou dost overthrow,
Die not, poore death, nor yet canst thou kill me.
From rest and sleepe, which but thy pictures bee,
Much pleasure, then from thee, much more must flow,
And soonest our best men with thee doe goe,
Rest of their bones, and soules deliverie.
Thou art slave to Fate, Chance, kings, and desperate men,
And dost with poyson, warre, and sicknesse dwell,
And poppie, or charmes can make us sleepe as well,
And better then thy stroake; why swell'st thou then;
One short sleepe past, wee wake eternally,
And death shall be no more; death, thou shalt die.

*John Donne*

# Thanatopsis

To him who in the love of nature holds
Communion with her visible forms, she speaks
A various language; for his gayer hours
She has a voice of gladness, and a smile
And eloquence of beauty; and she glides
Into his darker musings, with a mild
And healing sympathy that steals away
Their sharpness ere he is aware. When thoughts
Of the last bitter hour come like a blight
Over thy spirit, and sad images
Of the stern agony, and shroud, and pall,
And breathless darkness, and the narrow house,
Make thee to shudder, and grow sick at heart;—
Go forth, under the open sky, and list
To Nature's teachings, while from all around—
Earth and her waters, and the depths of air—
Comes a still voice. Yet a few days, and thee
The all-beholding sun shall see no more
In all his course; nor yet in the cold ground,
Where thy pale form was laid, with many tears,
Nor in the embrace of ocean, shall exist
Thy image. Earth, that nourished thee, shall claim
Thy growth, to be resolved to earth again,
And, lost each human trace, surrendering up
Thine individual being, shalt thou go
To mix forever with the elements,
To be a brother to the insensible rock
And to the sluggish clod, which the rude swain
Turns with his share, and treads upon. The oak
Shall send his roots abroad, and pierce thy mold.
Yet not to thine eternal resting-place
Shalt thou retire alone, nor couldst thou wish
Couch more magnificent. Thou shalt lie down
With patriarchs of the infant world — with kings,
The powerful of the earth — the wise, the good,
Fair forms, and hoary seers of ages past,
All in one mighty sepulchre. The hills

Rock-ribbed and ancient as the sun, — the vales
Stretching in pensive quietness between;
The venerable woods — rivers that move
In majesty, and the complaining brooks
That make the meadows green; and, poured round all,
Old Ocean's gray and melancholy waste,—
Are but the solemn decorations all
Of the great tomb of man. The golden sun,
The planets, all the infinite host of heaven,
Are shining on the sad abodes of death
Through the still lapse of ages. All that tread
The globe are but a handful to the tribes
That slumber in its bosom. — Take the wings
Of morning, pierce the Barcan wilderness,
Or lose thyself in the continuous woods
Where rolls the Oregon, and hears no sound,
Save his own dashings — yet the dead are there:
And millions in those solitudes, since first
The flight of years began, have laid them down
In their last sleep — the dead reign there alone.
So shalt thou rest — and what if thou withdraw
In silence from the living, and no friend
Take note of thy departure? All that breathe
Will share thy destiny. The gay will laugh
When thou art gone, the solemn brood of care
Plod on, and each one as before will chase
His favorite phantom; yet all these shall leave
Their mirth and their employments, and shall come
And make their bed with thee. As the long train
Of ages glides away, the sons of men—
The youth in life's fresh spring, and he who goes
In the full strength of years, matron and maid,
The speechless babe, and the gray-headed man—
Shall one by one be gathered to thy side,
By those, who in their turn, shall follow them.
So live, that when thy summons comes to join
The innumerable caravan, which moves
To that mysterious realm, where each shall take
His chamber in the silent halls of death,

Thou go not, like the quarry-slave at night,
Scourged to his dungeon, but, sustained and soothed
By an unfaltering trust, approach thy grave
Like one who wraps the drapery of his couch
About him, and lies down to pleasant dreams.

*William Cullen Bryant*

## The Sleep

Of all the thoughts of God that are
Borne inward unto souls afar,
Along the Psalmist's music deep,
Now tell me if that any is,
For gift or grace, surpassing this—
'He giveth His belovèd sleep'?

What would we give to our beloved?
The hero's heart to be unmoved,
The poet's star-tuned harp, to sweep,
The patriot's voice, to teach and rouse,
The monarch's crown, to light the brows?
He giveth His belovèd, sleep.

What do we give to our beloved?
A little faith all undisproved,
A little dust to overweep,
And bitter memories to make
The whole earth blasted for our sake.
He giveth His belovèd, sleep.

'Sleep soft, beloved!' we sometimes say,
But have no tune to charm away
Sad dreams that through the eye-lids creep.
But never doleful dream again
Shall break the happy slumber when
He giveth His belovèd, sleep.

O earth, so full of dreary noises!
O men, with wailing in your voices!
O delvèd gold, the wailers heap!
O strife, O curse, that o'er it fall!
God strikes a silence through you all,
He giveth His belovèd, sleep.

His dews drop mutely on the hill;
His cloud above it saileth still,
Though on its slope men sow and reap.
More softly than the dew is shed,

Or cloud is floated overhead,
He giveth His belovèd, sleep.

Aye, men may wonder while they scan
A living, thinking, feeling man
Confirmed in such a rest to keep;
But angels say, and through the word
I think their happy smile is heard—
'He giveth His belovèd, sleep.'

For me, my heart that erst did go
Most like a tired child at a show,
That sees through tears the mummers leap,
Would now its wearied vision close,
Would child-like on His love repose,
Who giveth His belovèd, sleep.

And, friends, dear friends,—when it shall be
That this low breath is gone from me,
And round my bier ye come to weep,
Let One, most loving of you all,
Say, 'Not a tear must o'er her fall;
He giveth His belovèd, sleep.'

*Elizabeth Barrett Browning*

## Postmortem

Having stood at the edge of a hole dug
As depositary for the body,
I.e., the mortal bit, blip on the screen,
Form given to us, form taken;

                  having stood
Thus, and watched it lowered, the big box
Waxed and shined to a faux-bronze finish,

I've found words to be shyer than they seem.
Pushed to the edge, they won't leap. In the shade
Of the valley of death, they're toy lamps; they pierce
The wily darkness not. Still,

Bless the nouns and verbs of prayer, the hymnal's
Stodgy rhymes, vanishing in the careless sky
That roofs the bereaved —

                any sound to efface
The syllable of wind jabbering in the ear,
And on fake metal, the thud of living rose.

*Clare Rossini*

## Nine Deaths

"Cancer is a series of deaths"
        *Georgia Newman*


### 1. Surgery

Late April. You've just learned
they will cut away your breast, or part of it.

We've cried,
discussed statistics,
told our children and friends.
We drive out
and walk in the green spring evening
hearing cows and birds, watching leafing trees.

"The world's so beautiful," I say. Or is that you?
We hold hands.
This is a death, the first,
and we can bear it.


### 2. Liver Scan

It's summer now. Your radiation's over.
In the last conference at the Cleveland Clinic
we get bad news:
a liver scan
shows two spots,
metastases,
the cancer erupting in a new place.

The chemo will have to be
much more severe.
The statistics he gives
are still encouraging
but hope has shrunk.
This is another death. We live
inside a tighter circle now.

All day we drive east.
Whenever I glance at you
your face is peaceful.
We listen to music, read the scenery,
fold and unfold our maps.
Oh this is a death, all right
As we head up
toward the Green Mountains.

### 3. Indefinitely

Now there's an interlude of nearly a year
in which there's no death, just some dying,
and most of it bearable.
We feel close and, often, happy,
lucky to have each other for the time,
and our two children, half adults.

You're not as able as you hoped.
You need to take my arm,
shaky in traffic and crowds,
tiring easily.
Sometimes your appetite is good,
sometimes you can't take much
except some tea and oatmeal.
Sometimes you throw up, again and again.

Now they change the regimen.
You ask your doctor
how long you'll be on this new set of drugs.
As long as they work
to keep those liver spots from spreading.
And then? And then a new set.
And how long on chemotherapy?
Indefinitely, he says.

It comes across us both,
a sickening dawn that we saw coming:
We can't expect to beat the disease.
It's June. Ripe summer has set in again.
This is a death.

*4. Seizure.*

One August night,
you wake me with your movements.
I try to help you up, but you fall, helpless,
hitting your face on the night-table.
Then come convulsions. Then unconsciousness.
Shaking, I summon the ambulance
and they take you to Emergency.
You have another seizure there.
Next day, CAT scan confirms the doctor's hunch:
two little tumors in the brain.
These can be treated with radiation, we're assured.
The real risk continues in the liver.

Gradually, gingerly,
we move back into our routines.
You have no memory of your seizure.
You often ask me about it.
I remember everything
too vividly: the horror of your fall,
my helplessness, your absence in convulsions
and unconsciousness.
It's taken me three months
to tell this part of the story.
That's how I know what a death is.
And yet our lives go on.

*5. Lung Spots*

September. A chest x-ray
is taken again.
There are two spots on the lung.

I know how much this sets you back
by how long it takes you to tell
your father and your children.

I don't know how much
you cry in the bathroom
or when I'm not around.

This is a little death, but it goes deep.

*6. Anemia*

You keep going to work.
Morning after morning,
dropping you off,
watching your slow movements,
I feel my heart
crack into contrary parts:
admiration for your courage,
sorrow for your slow decline.

Oh eating is death and hunger is death,
and I don't know, or won't admit it.
We drift through January, a rugged month,
and I make soups, brown rice and junkets.
Somehow the things you ate as a child,
your mother's bridge club casseroles
and thirties cooking,
help you most. You dwindle,
and we both try not to notice.
Finally, one early February night,
your breathing grows terribly labored.
The doctor admits you to the hospital for blood
        transfusions.
But there is something ominous in this.

*7. Heart Failure*

Your heart fails during the transfusion.
Weakened by medication, it can't drive
your damaged lungs.
Your breathing stops.
They rush you to Intensive Care
manage to revive you,
hooking you up to a breathing machine
that helps you—makes you?—go on living.
You never regain consciousness.
Three days we watch beside your bed,
talking to you, whispering, pleading.

I want to let you go. I want to keep you.
Where has your beauty gone,
your gaze, your poise and animation
What or whom am I standing beside?
What ears hear my whispers of love?

### 8. Unplug the Respirator

A scan shows you've probably been gone,
brain-dead,
since the heart first stopped.

Is this then the moment of death?
This is the eighth of nine.

### 9. She's Like a Painting/Bless Her Heart

At the last you look composed,
unhooked, released, at peace,
as we come in groups of two and three
to take our leave of you.
I can touch and kiss you again,
though your waxy stillness
tells me I'm kissing your husk.

My mind shoots like a bobsled
back through the whole course of the illness.
Once again, arm in arm,
summoning courage
we are walking out of the Cleveland Clinic…

One last look for us.
"She's like a painting," whispers Margaret
and that is true.

"Bless her heart," says my simple mother,
twice,
and those words are oddly right.

You're like a painting.

Bless your heart.

*10. Coda*

Your dreams are over.
My dreams begin.

In the first you are wearing a striped blouse
and vomiting in the kitchen sink.
I watch your back from a helpless distance.

In the second, helping you move to a chair
at some social gathering,
I realize you are lifeless
like a mummy or a dummy.

In the third, I arrive running, late,
for some graveside service.
You are waiting in the crowd, impatient and withdrawn.
But then you embrace me.
What a relief to touch you again!

These dreams are not your visits,
just my clumsy inventions.
I live in an empty house
with wilting flowers and spreading memories
and my own heart
that hollows and fills.
I'm addressing you
and you can't hear me.
If you can, you don't need
to be told this story.
I need to tell it to myself
until I can stand to hear it.

And you're not here
except in the vaguest ways.
Were you the hawk
that followed us back
from your memorial service
that brilliant winter day?

Are you the rabbit
I keep seeing
that's tamer than it should be?
I wish I could believe it.
You're none of these things or all of them.

What does Montale say?
Words from the oven, words from the freezer,
that's what poetry is.

This is neither.
This is an empty house and a heart
that hollows and fills, hollows and fills.

*Chloe Hamilton Young, 1927-1985*

*David Young*

## Reading the Obituary Page

In starched dresses
with ribbons
in miniature jackets
and tiny ties
we would circle
the chairs
at birthday parties and
when the music
stopped, lunge
to be seated. One
by one we were welcomed
to hard ground
and empty air.

*Linda Pastan*

# After the Funeral: Cleaning out the Medicine Cabinet

Behind this mirror no new world
opens to Alice. Instead, we find
the old world, rearranged in rows,
a dusty little chronicle
of small complaints and private sorrows,
each cough caught dry and airless
in amber, the sore feet powdered
and cool in their yellow can.
To this world turned the burning eyes
after their search, the weary back
after its lifting, the heavy heart
like an old dog, sniffing the lid
for an answer. Now one of us
unscrews the caps and tries the air
of each disease. Another puts
the booty in a shoe box: tins
of laxatives and aspirin,
the corn pads and the razor blades,
while still another takes the vials
of secret sorrows—the little pills
with faded, lonely codes—holding
them out the way one holds a spider
pinched in a tissue, and pours them down
the churning toilet and away.

*Ted Kooser*

## Dirge Without Music

I am not resigned to the shutting away of loving hearts in the
    hard ground.
So it is, and so it will be, for so it has been, time out of mind:
Into the darkness they go, the wise and the lovely. Crowned
With lilies and with laurel they go; but I am not resigned.

Lovers and thinkers, into the earth with you.
Be one with the dull, the indiscriminate dust.
A fragment of what you felt, of what you knew,
A formula, a phrase remains,—but the best is lost.

The answers quick and keen, the honest look, the laughter,
    the love,—
They are gone. They are gone to feed the roses. Elegant and
    curled
Is the blossom. Fragrant is the blossom. I know. But I do not
    approve.
More precious was the light in your eyes than all the roses in
    the world.

Down, down, down into the darkness of the grave
Gently they go, the beautiful, the tender, the kind;
Quietly they go, the intelligent, the witty, the brave.
I know. But I do not approve. And I am not resigned.

*Edna St. Vincent Millay*

## Dawn Revisited

Imagine you wake up
with a second chance: The blue jay
hawks his pretty wares
and the oak still stands, spreading
glorious shade. If you don't look back,

the future never happens.
How good to rise in sunlight,
in the prodigal smell of biscuits—
eggs and sausage on the grill.
The whole sky is yours

to write on, blown open
to a blank page. Come on,
shake a leg! You'll never know
who's down there, frying those eggs,
if you don't get up and see.

*Rita Dove*

Sick on a journey—
over parched fields
dreams wander on

*Matsuo Basho*

(translated by Lucien Stryke)

# So Big a Thing

## Tell Me

Tell me the night silence
on the locked Alzheimer's ward is broken
by a yell from room 206,

that an old man with flattened
nose and crumpled ears,
whose family moved away to Arizona,

whose doctor never comes
to visit, is standing
in the middle of that room, naked,

his freckled face a clenched fist,
urine and feces running
down his legs.

Then tell me that the fat one, twelve
years on the job,
working her second shift because

someone's *car won't start,*
comes with a pan
of warm water, a sponge and a towel;

how, back in bed, he
cries, *You know-*
*I'm in the ring tomorrow with Killer;*

how a tiny smile begins, how
her hand reaches out
to flick down his wild flame of hair.

Now tell me again
why you don't believe in angels.

*George Young*

## So Big a Thing

Why am I so serious today,
My only love? You ask, and I cannot exactly
Say; except that somewhere,
So far away
I'm tired with trying to imagine
That much distance, that much air
And land—
Time, too—
Listen.
Somewhere, so long ago
Who now would know,
A thought started coming,
Coming, and at last is here,
Is here; but is so big a thing, so like a moving
Cloud, yet, oh, so slowly
Moving, like a world
Of weather with great storms in it
That do not break, that do not strike—
My only love, it cannot be
That this huge weightless thing
Was meant for me,
This thought that isn't in words
And never will be, yet it started
Coming, coming, and at last
Is here.

*Mark Van Doren*

## A Friend's Illness

Sickness brought me this
Thought, in that scale of his:
Why should I be dismayed
Though flame had burned the whole
World as it were a coal,
Now I have seen it weighed
Against a soul?

*W. B. Yeats*

## At the Children's Hospital in Little Rock

Scorning the schemes of nature,
by accident, illness, and murder,
chance hands the past our future
and ruins us out of order.

We hope and beg as we can,
tugging the hem of frost
as if we were children again:
*Us first. Let us be first.*

*Miller Williams*

## In the Strand

Faces I see, as through the street I go,
Scarred by disease and sin that burn like fire,
And eyes with cold dead light of base desire,
Thin lips sucked in by self-absorption so
One scarce can tell if they are human or no,
Boys whose young candour dies within this mire,
Silly girl-faces that are fair for hire,
And over all a mesh of lies.

                I know
How taint of blood, gold-worship, passion's tide,
Curse of self-seeking, lovelessness of hell,
Do mould men's forms for ever as a glove
Is moulded by the living hand inside;
All this, I say, I know, and know as well,
I never knew a heart I might not love.

              *Havelock Ellis*

agonizing beyond words
this ailment
this hatred I feel
toward a pure maiden
totally unlike myself

*Yosano Akiko*

(translated by Makoto Ueda)

# Hope

It hovers in dark corners
before the lights are turned on,
   it shakes sleep from its eyes
   and drops from mushroom gills,
     it explodes in the starry heads
     of dandelions turned sages,
        it sticks to the wings of green angels
        that sail from the tops of maples.

It sprouts in each occluded eye
of the many-eyed potato,
   it lives in each earthworm segment
   surviving cruelty,
     it is the motion that runs
     from the eyes to the tail of a dog,
        it is the mouth that inflates the lungs
        of the child that has just been born.

It is the singular gift
we cannot destroy in ourselves,
the argument that refutes death,
the genius that invents the future,
all we know of God.

It is the serum which makes us swear
not to betray one another;
it is in this poem, trying to speak.

                    *Lisel Mueller*

## Communal Living

When we were young and immortal
what would we have said,
if an angel had come down
to our shack in Oregon's green
hills, as we warmed ourselves
beside the woodstove in a dark
soot-laden dawn, waiting for
Enid to make a pot of oatmeal,
Wayne to chop more wood;

if she waded her way among the piles
of duffel bags, the psychedelic
watercolors, the cans of Bugler,
packs of Camels with rising suns,
waves of color and stars drawn on,
found us in overalls and hiking boots,
our long cotton paisley skirts,
hair down past the waist, our manes
blowing in the smoky early morning
as we rolled our first cigarettes
or weed, maybe someone put on The Band,
Jackie Lomax or Fresh Cream.

She would furl her wings, point and
say—you, dead at 23, a suicide; you,
medical school; you, a life of loss and
unemployment; you, a mother, activist
in Vermont; you, filmmaker in Russia;
you, one year of law school, one son,
then dead at 40, an unnamed virus.
Would we have tilted back our
uncombed heads and laughed?

*Alice Jones*

fearing
what lies in my heart
may be heard

i quickly draw back my chest

from the stethoscope



forgetting
my illness for a moment

I try
to bellow like an ox—

before my wife and child come home



*Ishikawa Takuboku*

(translated by Makoto Ueda)

## Transplant

*The heart was harvested in Wisconsin*
*And flown in by helicopter.*
—Atlanta radio news

Within the green purpose of the room
there were ten beating hearts, but now are nine
who help the otherworldly pump assume
the flow of blood along the plastic line

by which the tenth now lives and has his being—
which is slow asleep, but dreams of moving,
of breathing on its own, of dimly seeing
its alien toes awake, all ten approving

the knitting of this widely opened chest—
where now there is no heart, but only pocket
until the circling mercy comes to rest
as neatly as an eye within its socket

and then the shock, the charmed expectant start,
the last astonished harvest of the heart.

*John Stone*

## HMO

*After Emerson's "Brahma"*

If, as Mother damply thanks midwife,
Neonate should think, "Sweet gift of life!",
Bless him, red and wheezing from hard strife,
Whose umbilicus whets my knife.

Anesthesia and shaving cream
Heal the scarred, scare the well-heeled,
And stain the white coats of selfless self-esteem
Hard cash anneals.

Such is the Condition Pre-Existent:
No man can raise decedent co-payees.
Thus I, to mourn the debtor and the debt,
Must waive some fees.

Yet ambulance, taxi, gurney, wheelchair,
Crutch, cane, strong arm of next of kin
Yield unto Kaiser what is Kaiser's—
To the last sovereign.

*Daniel Bosch*

## Mastectomy

the fall of
velvet plum points and umber aureolae

remember living

forget cool evening air kisses the rush of
liberation freed from the brassiere

forget the cupping of his hands the pleasure
his eyes looking down/anticipating

forget his mouth. his tongue at the nipples
his intense hungry nursing

forget sensations which begin either
on the right or the left. go thru the body
linger between thighs

forget the space once grasped during his ecstasy

*sweet sweet mama you taste so*

*Wanda Coleman*

## Here

Here I am in the garden laughing
an old woman with heavy breasts
and a nicely mapped face

how did this happen
well that's who I wanted to be

at last   a woman
in the old style   sitting
stout thighs apart under
a big skirt   grandchild sliding
on   off my lap   a pleasant
summer perspiration

that's my old man across the yard
he's talking to the meter reader
he's telling him the world's sad story
how electricity is oil or uranium
and so forth   I tell my grandson
run over to your grandpa   ask him
to sit beside me for a minute   I
am suddenly exhausted by my desire
to kiss his sweet explaining lips

*Grace Paley*

## The Sick Wife

The sick wife stayed in the car
while he bought a few groceries.
Not yet fifty,
she had learned what it's like
not to be able to button a button.

It was the middle of the day—
and so only mothers with small children
or retired couples
stepped through the muddy parking lot.

Dry cleaning swung and gleamed on hangers
in the cars of the prosperous.
How easily they moved—
with such freedom,
even the old and relatively infirm.

The windows began to steam up.
The cars on either side of her
pulled away so briskly
that it made her sick at heart.

*Jane Kenyon*

## Waving Good-Bye

I wanted to know what it was like before we
had voices and before we had bare fingers and before we
had minds to move us through our actions
and tears to help us over our feelings,
so I drove my daughter through the snow to meet her friend
and filled her car with suitcases and hugged her
as an animal would, pressing my forehead against her,
walking in circles, moaning, touching her cheek,
and turned my head after them as an animal would,
watching helplessly as they drove over the ruts,
her smiling face and her small hand just visible
over the giant pillows and coat hangers
as they made their turn into the empty highway.

*Gerald Stern*

## Birthday Card to My Mother

The toughness indoor people have:
    the will
to brave confusion in
mohair sofas, crocheted doilies—challenging
in every tidy corner some
bit of the outdoor drift and sag;
    the tenacity
in forty quarts of cherries up for winter,
gallon churns of sherbet at
family reunions,
fifty thousand suppers cleared away;
    the tempering
of rent-men at the front door, hanging on,
light bills overdue,
sons off to war or buried, daughters
taking on the names of strangers.

You have come through
the years of wheelchairs, loneliness—
a generation of pain
knotting the joints like ancient apple trees;
you always knew
this was no world to be weak in:
where best friends wither to old
phone numbers in far-off towns;
where the sting of children is always
sharper than serpents' teeth; where
love itself goes shifting
and slipping away to shadows.

You have survived it all,
come through wreckage and triumph hard
at the center but spreading
gentleness around you—nowhere
by your bright hearth has the dust
of bitterness lain unswept;
today, thinking back, thinking ahead
to other birthdays, I

lean upon your courage
and sign this card, as always,
with love.

*Philip Appleman*

## What the Body Told

Not long ago, I studied medicine.
It was terrible, what the body told.
I'd look inside another person's mouth,
And see the desolation of the world.
I'd see his genitals and think of sin.

Because my body speaks the stranger's language,
I've never understood those nods and stares.
My parents held me in their arms, and still
I think I've disappointed them; they care,
They stare and nod, they make their pilgrimage

To somewhere distant in my heart, they cry.
I look inside their other-person's mouths
And see the sleek interior of souls.
It's warm and red in there—like love, with teeth.
I've studied medicine until I cried

All night. Through certain books, a truth unfolds.
Anatomy and physiology,
The tiny sensing organs of the tongue—
Each nameless cell contributing its needs.
It was fabulous, what the body told.

*Rafael Campo*

## Relaxing in the Charity Ward at Mercy Hospital

All the old/men
        lie dying
squirming in their own shit
in the Hospital named Mercy

All the old/men
        lie dying
        all day dying
        in the morning dying

When the well/ fed/ pink cheeked priest
at break of day follows a white/ starched nun
thru the Charity / Welfare ward at the Hospital
named Mercy. The fat well fed priest
B
l
e
ss all the old/men who
        lie dying
squirming in their own shit

*Etheridge Knight*

## The Geriatric Ward

Bald this, hunched, jaw on fist,
or, ten-fingered, palps pate;
silent that, strains, leaning
to conjure monsters
from tap or counterpane.

Others rigid sit,
absent with empty eyes;
or, prone, sigh, call out,
at times cry quietly,
or moan continually.

One, at his own distance, nips
numb thumb and forefinger,
if he can grip it, at
saltcellar, napkin,
holding on to something.

*John Hewitt*

## The Very Old

The very old are forever
hurting themselves,

burning their fingers
on skillets, falling

loosely as trees
and breaking their hips

with muffled explosions of bone.
Down the block

they are wheeled in
out of our sight

for years at a time.
To make conversation,

the neighbors ask
if they are still alive.

Then, early one morning,
through our kitchen windows

we see them again,
first one and then another,

out in their gardens
on crutches and canes,

perennial,
checking their gauges for rain.

*Ted Kooser*

## Emigration

Try being sick for a year,
then having that year turn into two,
until the memory of your health is like an island
going out of sight behind you

and you sail on in twilight,
with the sound of waves.
It's not a dream. You pass
through waiting rooms and clinics

until the very sky seems pharmaceutical,
and the faces of the doctors are your stars
whose smile or frown
means to hurry and get well

or die.
And because illness feels like punishment,
an enormous effort to be good
comes out of you—
like the good behavior of a child

desperate to appease
the invisible parents of this world.
And when that fails,
there is an orb of anger

rising like the sun above
the mind afraid of death,
and then a lake of grief, staining everything below,
and then a holding action of neurotic vigilance

and then a recitation of the history
of second chances.
And the illusions keep on coming,
and fading out, and coming on again

while your skin turns yellow from the medicine,
your ankles swell like dough above your shoes,
and you stop wanting to make love
because there is no love in you,

only a desire to be done.
But you're not done.
Your bags are packed
and you are traveling.

*Tony Hoagland*

## To Those in the Limbo of Illness

You who have been here before,
Waiting,
Not knowing.

Not living,
Not dying.

Waiting

Waiting

While hope, the open wound,
Bleeds
Its life-giving
Life-exhausting
Blood.

In this limbo
Must love
Become an arc?

For the arc,
It has come to me,
Transcends
What it embraces.

*May Sarton*

## Impingement Syndrome

When one thing presses on another thing
and the result
is pain: could be in the shoulder,
elbow, knee, and the result is pain
and impaired movement.
It feels like pliers applied
to the bridge of your nose,
then wrenched. The result
is pain, in your body
or in your figurative heart.
Impingement: the bit-down jaws
of a gila monster (they won't let go),
a shark (they won't let go
until you're sawed in half).
Impingement: big toe
in the car door slammed,
the coffin lid you can't lift,
that which impedes movement
while causing pain
which impedes movement.
And to heal it
you push and pull over and over
at this angle and that, against it.
You will not be frozen,
not your shoulder,
or neck, or knees or heart,
you will not be frozen,
your range of movement made less, you will
whirl again your arms like a windmill.
your eye on the spot of pain
as it grows smaller: the entrance
to a cobra's burrow, then the eye of a spigot
that taps Satan's spine, until
it's the size of, and as deep as,
the final paragraph's last period's pinhead.

*Thomas Lux*

that hill
shaped like the breast
I have lost
will be adorned with
dead flowers in winter

*Nakajo Fumiko*
(translated by Makoto Ueda)

## The Urine Specimen

In the clinic, a sun-bleached shell of stone
on the shore of the city, you enter
the last small chamber, a little closet
chastened with pearl—cool, white, and glistening,
and over the chilly well of the toilet
you trickle your precious sum in a cup.
It's as simple as that. But the heat
of this gold your body's melted and poured out
into a form begins to enthrall you,
warming your hand with your flesh's fevers
in a terrible way. It's like holding
an organ—spleen or fatty pancreas,
a lobe from your foamy brain still steaming
with worry. You know that just outside
a nurse is waiting to cool it into a gel
and slice it onto a microscope slide
for the doctor, who in it will read your future,
wringing his hands. You lift the chalice and toast
the long life of your friend there in the mirror,
who wanly smiles, but does not drink to you.

*Ted Kooser*

## IV. Kelly

The patient is a twelve-year-old white female.
She's gravida zero, no STD's.
She'd never even had a pelvic. One
Month nausea and vomiting. No change
In bowel habits. No fever, chills, malaise.
Her school performance has been worsening.
She states that things at home are fine.
On physical exam, she cried but was
Cooperative. Her abdomen was soft,
With normal bowel sounds and question of
A suprapubic mass, which was non-tender.
Her pelvic was remarkable for scars
At six o'clock, no hymen visible,
Some uterine enlargement. Pregnancy
Tests positive times two. She says it was
Her dad. He's sitting in the waiting room.

*Rafael Campo*

## XI. Jane Doe #2

They found her unresponsive in the street
Beneath a lamplight I imagined made
Her seem angelic, regal even, clean.
She must have been around sixteen. She died
Who knows how many hours earlier
That day, the heroin inside her like
A vengeful dream about to be fulfilled.
Her hands were crossed about her chest, as though
Raised up in self-defense; I tried to pry
Them open to confirm the absence of
A heartbeat, but in death she was so strong,
As resolute as she was beautiful.
I traced the track marks on her arms instead,
Then pressed my thumb against her bloodless lips,
So urgent was my need to know. I felt
The quiet left by a departing soul.

*Rafael Campo*

## The Alien

I'm back again scrutinising the Milky Way
      of your ultrasound, scanning the dark
            matter, the nothingness, that now the heads say
      is chockablock with quarks & squarks,
gravitons & gravitini, photons & photinos. Our sprout,

who art there inside the spacecraft
      of your ma, the time capsule of this printout,
            hurling & whirling towards us, it's all daft
      on this earth. Our alien who art in the heavens,
our Martian, our little green man, we're anxious

to make contact, to ask divers questions
      about the heavendom you hail from, to discuss
            the whole shebang of the beginning&end,
      the pre-big-bang untime before you forget the why
and lie of thy first place. And, our friend,

to say Welcome, that we mean no harm, we'd die
      for you even, that we pray you're not here
            to subdue us, that we'd put away
      our ray guns, missiles, attitude and share
our world with you, little big head, if only you stay.

*Greg Delanty*

## Children's Hospital, Emergency Room

You do not want to be here
You wish it were you
The doctor is stitching up
It is a cut on the chin, fixable
This time but deep enough
To make you think of gashes
Puncture wounds flesh unfolding to the bone
Your child is lying on the table
Restrained, You must be still
The nurse who cradles her head is saying
And the doctor is embroidering
Delicately patiently like a kind aunt
But there is not enough solace in that
To make you stop thinking of other children
Whose hurt blooms like a dark interior bruise
In other rooms there is hysteria
The sound of glass shattering
And in the next bay there is the child
Who is sleeping too soundly
You do not want to hear such silence
The evidence which convicts, puts away
Wake up, you whisper, wake up
You want to think of water
A surface with no scars
You want the perpetuity of circles
A horizon clear and unbroken
And the sky a flat blue immensity
Without sides or depth
But there is nothing you can do
When your daughter calls out It hurts
And things regain their angularity
The vulnerable opaqueness, I'm here
You say, Be still, I'm here

*Gregory Djanikian*

## Vanishing Lung Syndrome

Once in a while somebody fights for breath.
He stops, getting in everyone's way.
The crowd flows around, muttering
about the flow of crowds,
but he just fights for breath.

Inside there may be growing
a sea monster within a sea monster,
a black, talking bird,
a raven Nevermore that
can't find a bust of Athena
to perch on and so just grows
like a bullous emphysema with cyst development,
fibrous masses and lung hypertension.

Inside there may be growing
a huge muteness of fairy tales,
the wood-block baby that gobbles up everything,
father, mother, flock of sheep,
dead-end road among fields,
screeching wagon and horse,
I've eaten them all and now I'll eat you,
while scintigraphy shows
a disappearance of perfusion, and angiography
shows remnants of arterial branches
without the capillary phase.

Inside there may be growing
an abandoned room,
bare walls, pale squares where pictures hung,
a disconnected phone,
feathers settling on the floor
the Encyclopedists have moved out and
Dostoevsky never found the place,

lost in the landscape
where only surgeons
write poems.

*Miroslav Holub*

## A Prayer of Anger

No hymn of praise today.
No hand-clapping alleluia

*For the All-good God*
And his marvelous handiwork.
    Lord
    A child has been born bad.
    He gangles and twitches and shames
The undiscovered galaxies of your creation.
Why could not the hands
    that strung the stars
Dip into that womb to bless and heal?

Please no voice from Job's Whirlwind
Saying how dare I.       I dare!
    Yet I know no answer comes
    Save that tears dry up, skin knits,
    And humans love broken things.
But to you who are always making pacts
You have my word on this —
On the final day of fire
After You have stripped me
(if there is breath left)
I will subpoena You to the stand
In the court of human pain.

*John Shea*

## Snapshot of a Lump

I imagine Nice and topless beaches,
women smoking and reading novels in the sun.
I pretend I am comfortable undressing
in front of men who go home to their wives,
in front of women who have seen
    twenty pairs of breasts today,
in front of silent ghosts who walked
    through these same doors before me,
who hoped doctors would find it soon enough,
    that surgery, pills and chemo could save them.

Today, they target my lump
with a small round sticker, a metal capsule
embedded beneath clear plastic.
I am asked to wash off my deodorant,
wrap a lead apron around my waist,
pose for the nurse, for the white walls—
one arm resting on the mammogram machine,
that "come hither" look in my eyes.
*This is my first time being photographed topless.*
I tell the nurse, *Will I be the centerfold*
*or just another playmate?*

My breast is pressed flat—a torpedo,
a pyramid, a triangle, a rocket on this altar;
this can't be good for anyone.
Finally, the nurse, winded
from fumbling, smiles,
says, "Don't breathe or move."
A flash and my breast is free,
but only for a moment.

In the waiting room, I sit between magazines,
an article on Venice,
health charts, people in white.
I pretend I am comfortable watching
other women escorted off to a side room,
where results are given with condolences.

I imagine leaving here
      with negative results and returned lives.
I imagine future trips to France,
      to novels I will write and days spent
beneath a blue and white umbrella,
waves washing against the shore like promises.

*Kelli Russell Agodon*

## poem to my uterus

you uterus
you have been patient
as a sock
while i have slippered into you
my dead and living children
now
they want to cut you out
stocking i will not need
where i am going
where am i going
old girl
without you
uterus
my bloody print
my estrogen kitchen
my black bag of desire
where can i go
barefoot
without you
where can you go
without me

*Lucille Clifton*

## The Psychiatrist Says She's Severely Demented

But she's my mother. She lies in her bed,
*Hi Sweetie,* she says.
*Hi Mom. Do you know my name?*
I can't wait for her answer, *I'm Bobbi.*
*Oh, so you found me again,* she says.
Her face and hair have the same gray sheen
Like a black and white drawing smudged on the edges.
The bedspread is hot pink, lime green. Her eyes,
Such a distant blue, indifferent as the sky. I put my hand
On her forehead. It is soft, and she resembles my real mother
Who I have not spoken to in so many years.
I want to talk to her as her eyes close.
She is mumbling something, laughing to herself,
All the sadness she ever had has fled.
And when she opens her eyes again, she stares through me
And her eyes well up with tears.
And I stand there lost in her incoherence,
Which feels almost exactly like love.

*Bobbi Lurie*

## Bypass

When they cracked open your chest, parting
the flesh at the sternum and sawing

right through your ribs, we'd been married
only five weeks. I had not yet kissed

into memory those places they raided
to save your life. I could only wait

outside, in the public lobby
of private nightmares

while they pried you apart, stopped
your heart's beating, and iced you

down. For seven hours a machine
breathed for you, in and out. God,

seeing you naked in ICU minutes
after the surgery… your torso swabbed

a hideous antiseptic yellow
around a raw black ladder of stitches

and dried blood. Still unconscious,
you did the death rattle on the gurney.

"His body is trying to warm itself up,"
they explained, to comfort me.

*Susan Kelly-DeWitt*

## 1 in 300

To lose at science is the accident of trying,
for worse or, best, acceptable ways cells divide

then swell into heart, spleen, spine
for every satisfaction, and love also aligned

according to sense. To carry a child
inside the shaky side of feeling wild

about it, to feel the shape of him
in inches lengthen, his heartbeat a hymn

that life can be taught without knowing
a thing, with all the opinions he, growing

older, would naturally form, based, again,
on chromosomes that deal out death and gain

like just another round at a half-lit table
of weary players hoping their hand is not terrible

as mine was. Little is given. Chance
is a mindless science too accurate to withstand.

*Diane Mehta*

## Hemophilia/Los Angeles

And so it circulates
from the San Bernardino Freeway
to the Santa Monica Freeway and
down to the San Diego Freeway and
up to the Golden Gate Freeway,

and so it circulates
in the vessels of the marine creature,
transparent creature,
unbelievable creature in the light
of the southern moon
like the footprint
of the last foot in the world,

and so it circulates
as if there were no other music
except Perpetual Motion,
as if there were no conductor
directing an orchestra of black angels
without a full score:

out of the grand piano floats
a pink C-sharp in the upper octave,
out of the violin
blood may trickle at any time,
and in the joints of the trombone
there swells a fear of the tiniest staccato,

as if there were no Dante
in a wheelchair,
holding a ball of cotton to his mouth,
afraid to speak a line
lest he perforate the meaning,

as if there were no genes
except the gene for defects
and emergency telephone calls,

and so it circulates
with the full, velvet hum of the disease,

circulates all hours of the day,
circulates all hours of the night
to the praise of non-clotting,

each blood cell carrying
four molecules of hope
that it might all be something
totally different
from what it is.

*Miroslav Holub*

## Enter Patient

(Part I of *In Hospital*)

THE morning mists still haunt the stony street;
The northern summer air is shrill and cold;
And lo, the Hospital, grey, quiet, old,
Where Life and Death like friendly chafferers meet.
Thro' the loud spaciousness and draughty gloom
A small, strange child — o aged yet so young! —
Her little arm besplinted and beslung,
Precedes me gravely to the waiting-room.
I limp behind, my confidence all gone.
The grey-haired soldier-porter waves me on,
And on I crawl, and still my spirits fail:
tragic meanness seems so to environ
These corridors and stairs of stone and iron,
Cold, naked, clean — half-workhouse and half jail.

*William Ernest Henley*

## Parkinson's Disease

You greet me
with shaking hands
and no smile
on your face.

You shuffle
through dead leaves,
or falling, run
to catch yourself up.

Arms never swing,
but restless fingers
roll the seconds
into pills.

You stoop
to look for yourself,
eyes lost
in caves of bone.

'What's happening?'
leaks out
with the moisture
from your mouth.

A monochrome voice,
the film frozen
on the screen
of your face.

The equipment
broken.
The projectionist
gone home.

*Christopher J. Woods*

## The Doctor's Wife

Years later she came to me
for a menagerie of shots
and some advice on water
in New Guinea. It didn't take
a minute to notice the tic
that sprung up since the last
bout of whatever her illness was
and the devastated nails.
Her church was sending her
for three months, maybe six,
to a site on the north coast
where thousands of refugees
had fled to escape a war
on the next island, a conflict
that hadn't made the news
so far. They needed a nurse
more than a preacher, but she
volunteered for both. I wished
we had more time to talk
that morning. Her waxen aura
was singular, like speaking
to a statue by candlelight -
it's hard to explain. The church
was sending a team with her,
plus some outdated medicines
from the clinic. She withdrew
her eyes from my desk at last
and whispered, *He always wished
to do God's work in the missions,
didn't he?* I had never met
the man. He placed that bullet
in his head before I came
to town. I knew the handwriting
that he used to cure the sick, though,
and the once-vivid stories
of his compassion. *He's looking
over your shoulder in this,*
I said. *Remember that.*

*Jack Coulehan*

## Prayer

Send rain, down to the dry bare bones of me,
   the tarsals planted in sand, no sage
   or mint or parsley will grow here, snails
   are sucked dry, leave frail shells
   in the dug garden's dirt, no flowers, no fronds;

Send rain, down to the deep bowl of my pelvis,
   barren red hollow, the empty sack
   sags now with age, the scarred yellow ovals
   discharge their eggs in irregular cycles,
   no longer linked so well to the moon;

Send rain, down to the restless quartered meat
   that thuds on my ribs, whose valves
   measure thin blood as it seeps through
   the pipes feeding desiccated organs,
   whose mortal work forms sludge;

Send rain, down to the small transparent curve,
   the opaque lens that filters dim light
   to the lustrous surface and on to dense
   convolutions of brain, the task of my sighted
   vitreous globes that turn in their padded cells;

Send rain, down to the knots and whorls,
   where memory continues to pile its thick layers
   sloughs surface, and roots reach into
   that grey ground where my neurons grow sparse
   and leached soil sprouts nothing new.

Send rain.

*Alice Jones*

## Captain

A country-man at heart.
Shrewd, sensitive. Big,
One would even say:
Enormous.

Pain wrecks a man.

A ship on craggy rocks.
Weatherbeaten by life,
Chest forward,
Lone Mast,
Torn Joints.
Pain — Movement.
Sails on against
Wind and waves
Slowly.
Groaning — a little.
A little afraid
A lot in need
Of being helped
Silently.

Younger ships
Younger crew
Silently
Move forward with

An Old man of the Sea.

*Miriam Kennedy*

## Theodosus Bull
*Delirium Tremens*

You walked in off Howard
And told of two fifths a day
And we didn't believe you—
      Until you belched blood
          and the Aid fainted.

And you wept dry tears
To see the technicolor worms
Shucking your skull like a rotten pecan
And we didn't believe you—
      Until you stuck your head
          through the window pane.

And you mumbled of rats and riots
And drinking after-shave lotion
And your kid in the can
And we didn't believe you—
      Until we scraped off your socks.

And you babbled on about
The injustices you'd suffered at the
Hands of society
And we didn't believe you—
      Until the night nurse found you hanging
          peacefully by your neck
          from the saliva aspirator.

*K. D. Beernink*

```
      P
      A
      T
      H
R E P O R T
      L
      O
      G
      Y
```

| | |
|---|---|
| The specimens | Parts of me |
| are received | cut from their moorings |
| in two containers | floating placidly |
| specimen No. 1 | lifted out |
| labeled | by dispassionate hands |
| ovary | measured, weighe |
| the external surface | splayed on a counter |
| distorted | so much |
| by a large | once secret |
| cystic structure | now exposed |
| filled with | old |
| dark | imperfections |
| reddish-brown | festering |
| material | like a failed heart |
| specimen No. 2 | large, scarred |
| labeled | utterly useless |
| uterus | no matter that |
| opening reveals | a creation of sorts |
| a mass | suggestive of life |
| with fleshy-pink | formed |
| whorled surface | inside |
| the cavity | which |
| is compressed | at last |
| by the mass | cut to the quick |
| representative sections | proved counterfeit |
| are submitted | stillborn |

*Veneta Masson*

## The Almond Tree
### *Jonathan: 1965*

I

All the way to the hospital
The lights were green as peppermints.
Trees of black iron broke into leaf
ahead of me, as if
I were the lucky prince
in an enchanted wood
summoning summer with my whistle,
banishing winter with a nod.

Swung by the road from bend to bend,
I was aware that blood was running
down through the delta of my wrist
and under arches
of bright bone. Centuries,
continents it had crossed;
from an undisclosed beginning
spiraling to an unmapped end.

II

Crossing (at sixty) Magdalen Bridge
Let it be a son, a son, said
the man in the driving mirror,
Let it be a son. The tower
held up its hand: the college
bells shook their blessings on his head.

III

I parked in an almond's
shadow blossom, for the tree
was waving, waving at me
upstairs with a child's hands.

IV

Up
the spinal stair
and at the top
along
a bone-white corridor
the blood tide swung
me swung me to a room
whose walls shuddered
with the shuddering womb.
Under the sheet
wave after wave, wave
after wave beat
on the bone coast,
bringing ashore — whom?
New-
minted, my bright farthing!
Coined by our love, stamped
With our images, how you
Enrich us! Both
you make one. Welcome
to your white sheet,
my best poem.

V

At seven-thirty
the visitors' bell
scissored the calm
of the corridors.
The doctor walked with
to the slicing doors.
His hand is upon my arm,
his voice — I have to tell
you — set another bell
beating in my head:
your son is a Mongol
the doctor said.

VI

How easily the word went in —
clean as a bullet
leaving no mark on the skin,
stopping the heart within it.

This was my first death.
The 'I' ascending on a slow
Last thermal breath
studied the man below

as a pilot treading air might
the buckled shell of his plane —
boot, glove and helmet
feeling no pain

from the snapped wires' radiant ends.
Looking down from a thousand feet
I held four walls in the lens
of an eye; wall, window, the street

a torrent of windscreens, my own
car under its almond tree,
and the almond waving me down.
I wrestled against gravity,

but light was melting and the gulf
cracked open. Unfamiliar
the body of my late self
I carried to the car.

VII

The hospital — its heavy freight
lashed down ship-shape ward over ward —
steamed into night with some on board
soon to be lost if the desperate

charts were known. Others would come
altered to land or find the land
altered. At their voyage's end
some would be added to, some

diminished. In a numbered cot
my son sailed from me; never to come
ashore into my kingdom
speaking my language. Better not

look that way. The almond tree
was beautiful in labour. Blood-
dark, quickening, bud after bud
split, flower after flower shook free.

On the darkening wind a pale
face floated. Out of reach. Only when
the buds, all the buds were broken
would the tree be in full sail.

In labour the tree was becoming
itself. I, too, rooted in earth
and ringed by darkness, from the death
of myself saw myself blossoming,

wrenched from the caul of my thirty
years' growing, fathered by my son,
unkindly in a kind season
by love shattered and set free.

*Jon Stallworthy*

## Heart Transplant

After an hour

there's an abyss in the chest
created by the missing heart
like a model landscape
where humans have grown extinct.

The drums of extracorporeal circulation
introduce
an inaudible
New World Symphony.

It's like falling from an airplane, the air growing
    cooler and cooler,
until it condenses in the inevitable moonlight,
the clouds coming closer, below the left foot, below
    the right foot,
a microscopic landscape with roads like capillaries
pulsing in counter-movements,
feeble hands grasping for the King of Blood,
"Seek the Lord while he may be found,"
ears ringing with the whistles of some kind of cosmic
    marmots,
an indifferent bat's membrane spreading between the
    nerves,
"It is unworthy of great hearts to broadcast their own
    confusion."

It's like falling from an airplane
before the masked face of a creator
ho's dressed in a scrub suit
and latex gloves.

Now they are bringing, bedded in melting ice,
the new heart,
like some trophy
from the Eightieth Olympiad of Calamities.

Atrium is sewn to atrium,
aorta to aorta,
three hours of eternity
coming and going.

And when the heart begins to beat
and the curves jump
like synthetic sheep
on the green screen,
it's like a model of a battlefield
where Life and Spirit
have been fighting
and both have won.

*Miroslav Holub*

## *From* **Sad Playthings**

How is it that the nurse's hand
    Which feels my pulse seems, strange to say,
So warm one day, and then so cold,
    And also hard another day?

*Ishikawa Takuboku*

(translated by H.H. Honda)

## The Nursing Home

There are more women than
men in the nursing home and
more men than old doctors.

Staff doctors visit once a
month. The few old men do
very little but sleep. Two

or three of them occasionally
gather outside in clear
weather for a smoke, which

is allowed them. I suppose
those in charge feel that
it can make no difference

now, and it brings the old
men a little pleasure. I
sit and chat with them

sometimes. Perhaps "chat"
is a bit too lively a word
to describe what passes for

conversation during these
puffing sessions. A lot
of low grunting goes on.

There is one old man who
is afflicted with bone
cancer and who says, in

high good humor, that his
guarantees have run out.
He was a traveling salesman

in women's wear, and still
remembers how much he loved
women. Many of the women

have become little girls
again. They carry dolls
about with them, mostly

rag-dolls, I suppose so
they can't injure themselves
when they squeeze them.

To see these toothless,
balding old ladies, frail
as twigs, clutching these dolls,

is heartbreaking. Oh, to love
something! It's still there.
It has been in them since

they were little and had dirty
knees and bows in their hair.
Some recognize me now, and,

when I give them a wave,
they wave back. It's a
wonderful feeling to make

contact, but it is difficult
to tell how much they know.
The care-givers are kind and

efficient. They are mostly
young, and apparently try
to imbue the old with some of

their zest for life, but
of course the old know all
that already—or knew and have

forgotten it. I wonder,
can the young reverse their
situations with the old

and see themselves looking up
at such fresh faces from the
vantage of bed or wheelchair

or walker? I am too young
to join the old here in the
nursing home, this metaphor

(or is it the tenor of a
metaphor?) for the last days,
but I am too old

to feel the buoyancy of the
young; so, at least for the
context of the nursing home,

I have arrived at yet another
awkward age. After visiting
my mother, who is only partly

present, I go out and sit
with the old men and have a
smoke. We hope for clear days.

*E. M. Schorb*

# Mad Farmers and Homeopathic Blues

## Manifesto: The Mad Farmer Liberation Front

Love the quick profit, the annual raise,
vacation with pay. Want more
of everything ready-made. Be afraid
to know your neighbors and to die.

And you will have a window in your head.
Not even your future will be a mystery
any more. Your mind will be punched in a card
and shut away in a little drawer.

When they want you to buy something
they will call you. When they want you
to die for profit they will let you know.
So, friends, every day do something
that won't compute. Love the Lord.
Love the world. Work for nothing.
Take all that you have and be poor.
Love someone who does not deserve it.

Denounce the government and embrace
the flag. Hope to live in that free
republic for which it stands.
Give your approval to all you cannot
understand. Praise ignorance, for what man
has not encountered he has not destroyed.

Ask the questions that have no answers.
Invest in the millenium. Plant sequoias.
Say that your main crop is the forest
that you did not plant,
that you will not live to harvest.

Say that the leaves are harvested
when they have rotted into the mold.
Call that profit. Prophesy such returns.
Put your faith in the two inches of humus
that will build under the trees
every thousand years.

Listen to carrion — put your ear
close, and hear the faint chattering
of the songs that are to come.
Expect the end of the world. Laugh.
Laughter is immeasurable. Be joyful
though you have considered all the facts.
So long as women do not go cheap
for power, please women more than men.

Ask yourself: Will this satisfy
a woman satisfied to bear a child?
Will this disturb the sleep
of a woman near to giving birth?

Go with your love to the fields.
Lie down in the shade. Rest your head
in her lap. Swear allegiance
to what is nighest your thoughts.

As soon as the generals and the politicos
can predict the motions of your mind,
lose it. Leave it as a sign
to mark the false trail, the way
you didn't go.

Be like the fox
who makes more tracks than necessary,
some in the wrong direction.
Practice resurrection.

*Wendell Berry*

## Homeopathic Blues in J.

Jones took the little daily dose
    Of Kruschen in his tea,
And cleaned his teeth with Pepsodent,
    That filmless they might be.

And when J. went to bed at night
    He left his windows wide,
And slept not on his back, for J.
    Preferred to on his side.

Again, J.'d take a dose of salts
    On rising from his bed,
And if he'd not a sixpenny bit
    Six pennies served instead.

J. had a little bread-and-milk,
    Some Liver Oil and malt,
And finished off his breakfast with
    An 'Andrews' Liver Salt.'

Concerning J. had I the art,
    I might for ever sing,
If only J.'d not just succumbed
    To septic poisoning.

*Malcolm Lowry*

## Hypochondriac Logic

Appendicitis is his worst
Obsession, mordant from the first
And unannounced. For who but he,
By curious failing schooled to see
The tiniest pain, can hope to be
Fore-warned of appendectomy?
So thinking, he thinks pain to be
More real as more illusory.

So argue all men who have thought
A truth more true as more remote,
Or in poetic worlds confide
The more their air is rarefied.
This the Shelleyan failing is,
Who feared elephantiasis,
Whose poems infect his readers too,
Who, since they're vague, suppose them true.

But lagging down a crippled street
Like fugitives from their own feet,
Some who are whole can yet observe
Disease is what we all deserve,
Or else disdain a painless life
While any squeal beneath the knife.
So, if you trace the impulse back,
The best are hypochondriac.

So poets may astonish you
With what is not, but should be, true,
And shackle on a moral shape
You only thought you could escape;
And if their scenery is queer,
Its prototype may not be here,
Unless inside a frightened mind,
Which may be dazzled, but not blind.

*Donald Davie*

## The Physiology of Joy

In the bleakest centers of the body, researchers
have discovered tiny pockets of joy,
like the undersized bubbles that cling
to the corners of parched mouths.

We're trying to understand, the spokesman said.
He was staring into the camera. They might be
an immune system response to pain
or evidence that joy
in order to be released
must coalesce to a critical mass.
Then he leaned into our living room
to confide

that in his college anatomy class,
sometimes the bodies would sigh
at the end of a long dissection,
an unaccountable flutter under his hands.
Once he was last one out
of that blue gymnasium of a laboratory.
I don't know if it's proof, he said,

but when I switched off the lights
the transom windows glowed.

*Kathleen Flenniken*

## It's a Living

it's called customer service
trying to help my fellow man
make sense of the medical insurance
some slick carpetbagging agent
talked him into buying

there are no easy answers
like today
the guy on the phone
was speaking with restraint
holding on to his dignity
but i know begging when i hear it
his voice cracked as he told me
the doctor tending to his dying wife
was getting phone calls from one
of our case managers
being pressured to get her
released from the hospital

please he said
please ask them to stop
she's in so much pain
my wife my best friend
she's in a lot of pain and
there's nothing they can do
please stop the phone calls

i tell him he's got us mixed up
with someone else
there is no record
of any phone calls
in his wife's file
but i know better

i want to put him on hold
go find the sterile room with
white walls where faceless people
hold jelly donuts gripped
tight in their pudgy hands

as they put dollar signs
on the way we die

i want to stick my head inside
remind them that
sooner or later we all
finish the race
sometimes it ain't too pretty
but in the end
if we're lucky
we'll have the love
of a precious few
maybe the ability to stare
death in the eye
so let this one go
just leave her be

but instead i assure
the guy i'll do my best
to find out what's going on
wait for him to hang up
decide to take my break
10 minutes early

times like this i wish
i'd taken up smoking

*Richard Vargas*

## Autopsy

This is the sky where it meets
the water's surface.

This is the wet ridge of it,
the line between life and drowning.

This is the glow of embers rising
against the rigors of evergreen.

This is a ring of large stones,
and in the nostrils, cedar burning.

This is the sound, still throbbing
in the ear canal, of translucence

passing through narrow tubes.
This is the salt of confluence,

and the sweet of imperfection.
This is melody, harmony, silence.

And this —

is the dead space, the rift
behind the gums, that hollow.

*Virginia M. Heatter*

## Echocardiogram

How does, how does, how does it work
so, little valve stretching messily open, as wide as possible,
all directions at once, sucking air, sucking blood, sucking
                                        air-in-blood
how? On the screen I see the part of me that always
                                loves my life,
never tires
of what it takes, this in-and-out, this open-and-shut
                                in the dark chest of me,
tireless, without muscle or bone, all flex and flux and blind
will, little mouth widening, opening and opening and,
                                then snapping
shut, shuddering anemone entirely of darkness, sea creature
of the spangled and sparkling sea, down, down where light
                                cannot reach.
When the technician stoops, flips a switch, the most
                                unpopular kid in the class
stands offstage with a metal sheet, shaking it while Lear raves. So
this is the house where love lives, a tin shed in a windstorm, tin
shed at the sea's edge, the land's edge,
waters wild and steady, wild and steady, wild.

*Suzanne Cleary*

## Cancer Prayer

DOCTOR:

Tell me please, how to be cavalier
after twenty years of treating patients
with arrogant adjectives, with verbs
too powerful to be comprehensible,
and nouns with such innocent sounds —
*lymphoma, melanoma, breast
cancer* — that they shatter my ears.

Hope is sometimes a puddle
of stale rainwater for a parched mouth,
though I must continue to pray.

I pray that the power that makes genetic strands
proliferate aberrantly allows us to reverse it,
to discover a gene insertion to correct
each untoward event, and if not, then just today,
I pray that the little boy with Wilm's tumor
will have no side effects from his chemotherapy,
that this one woman with ovary cancer

in room 1122, will have a complete remission.
The word *cure*, dear God, is always
near my lips, though I have been constrained from
saying it aloud. Allow me at least to think it.

*Marc J. Straus*

## *From* **The Doctor's Dream**

I had a dream, and in that dream
    I thought that I had passed
Into that realm of blissful rest
    That doctors reach at last.

I dreamed of all the ups and downs
    Of thirty years of practice,
That brought with many a scented rose,
    Its compensating cactus.

…About the doctors and their bills,
    The good and bad we did,
The lives our skill so often saved,
    Mistakes the earth had hid.

The strictures on our moral worth,
    The sins we do commit,
And universal dump we get,
    By wholesale in the pit.

For many hold 'twould be so hard
    Through Heaven's gate to wheedle
A doctor as to drive a camel through
    A hypodermic needle.

Yet in my dream there seemed to be
    Misapprehension here;
For I felt sure physicians will
    Among the saints appear.

…For from the fount from whence they're cleansed,
    E'en doctors may come clean;
God gives to no exclusive class
    The power to enter in.

…And thus I dreamt that round me stood
    The victims of disease,
The patients I had failed to cure,
    Though some had paid my fees.

One said, "It is a happy place,
    My bliss is unalloyed;
Through your mistakes just ten years more
    Of Heaven I have enjoyed."

...Another made this queer complaint;
    "I'm prematurely sent;
The bungling doctors got me here
    Before development.

"I'm filled with love, my joy overflows,
    But what I most regret,
On earth I should have staid and got
    Capacity for it."

I here got shaky in my shoes,
    And asked if they'd attack us,
And raise a rumpus in these courts,
    With questions of malpractice.

"Oh, no!" he said, "there's no redress,
    No righting this affliction:
For courts are not in session here
    For want of jurisdiction.

"And if they were, in our behalf
    We must ourselves appear;
A first-class lawyer can't be had,
    I never found one here."...

*William Snowden Battles*

## Hospital Haiku

The new interns
        Stiff in starched white suits.
The July heat!


                                        Grinning into
                                                The newborn nursery
                                        A man holding daisies.


Screaming objections
        In the hospital lobby—
A small naked boy.


                                        All night below zero.
                                                Today in the clinic
                                        New complaints of chest pain.

Resting on the stairs
        An old man with a large chest
And a cigarette.


                        Holding daffodils
                                Near the hospital florist—
                        An old woman, weeping.



Only one room is lit
        In the hospital tonight—
And the August moon!



                        Beside this death bed
                                Two old men
                        Embracing.


                        *K. D. Beernink*

## To Stammering

Where did you come from, lamentable quality?
Before I had a life you were about to ruin my life.
The mystery of this stays with me.
"Don't brood about things," my elders said.
I hadn't any other experience of enemies from inside.
They were all from outside—big boys
Who cursed me and hit me; motorists; falling trees.
All these you were as bad as, yet inside. When I spoke, you were
     there.
I could avoid you by singing or by acting.
I acted in school plays but was no good at singing.
Immediately after the play you were there again.
You ruined the cast party.
You were not a sign of confidence.
You were not a sign of manliness.
You were stronger than good luck and bad; you survived the
     both.
You were slowly edged out of my throat by psychoanalysis
You who had been brought in, it seems, like a hired thug
To beat up both sides and distract them
From the main issue: oedipal love. You were horrible!
Tell them, now that you're back in your thug country,
That you don't have to be so rough next time you're called in
But can be milder and have the same effect—unhappiness and
     pain

*Kenneth Koch*

## Ruminations On a Technical Paper

*Rumble B, et al. Amyloid A4 protein and its precursor in Down's syndrome and Alzheimer's disease. N Engl J Med. 320:1446, 1989.*

**Abstract:** In patients with Alzheimer's disease, amyloid fibrils that are aggregates of A4 protein subunits are deposited in the brain. A similar process occurs at an earlier stage in persons with Down's syndrome. To investigate the deposition of amyloid in these diseases, we used a radioimmunoassay to measure levels of the amyloid precursor (PreA4) In the serum of 17 patients with Down's syndrome, 15 patients with Alzheimer's disease, and 33 normal elderly controls.

The mean (+/- SD) concentration of serum PreA4 was increased 1.5-fold in patients with Down's syndrome…. as compared with that in controls; the levels in patients with Alzheimer's disease were similar to those in controls. We also found that the concentration of PreA4 in the brain tissue of two adults with Down's syndrome (100 and 190 pmol per gram) was higher than in the brain tissue of either 26 patients with Alzheimer's disease (64.4 +/- 17.3 pmol per gram) or 17 elderly controls with neurological disease (68.5)…. Immuno-cyto-chemical studies of brain tissue from 26 patients with Down's syndrome showed that the deposition of A4 protein amyloid began in these patients approximately 50 years earlier than it began in 127 normal aging subjects studied previously, although the rate of deposition was the same.

We conclude that, since the gene for PreA4 is on the long arm of chromosome 21, which is present in triplicate in Down's syndrome, overexpression of this gene may lead to increased levels of PreA4 and amyloid deposition in Down's syndrome. However, since increased levels of PreA4 are not present in Alzheimer's disease, additional factors must account for the amyloid deposition in that disorder.

I. The Journal's Abstract, Suitably Condensed

In patients with Alzheimer's disease
amyloid fibrils that are aggregates
of A4 protein subunits are
deposited in the brain.

A similar process occurs at an earlier age
in persons with Down's syndrome. To
investigate the deposition of
amyloid in these diseases,

we used a radioimmunoassay to measure
levels of the amyloid precursor (PreA4)
in the serum of 17 patients
with Down's syndrome....

We conclude that....overexpression
of this gene may lead to increased levels
and amyloid deposition in Down's.
However, since

increased levels of PreA4 are not
present in Alzheimer's disease
additional factors must account....
for that disorder.


II. The Newspaper Version

The thought police have invaded the ectodomains
of preA4. They have built roadblocks and
    searched the   the trains
for static movements which might miss
the numbers carved on a boomerang
by eight et als and Kang
in a code of blot analysis.

And they have found the traitors, the saboteurs,
the Congo reds, the argyrophilic conspirators.
They are standing now under bare bulbs
devoid of neuritic change, confessing
to genetic overexpressing.

667 to 676 drop chins in a hangdog cluster.
They have arrested Creutzfeldt-Jacob, Straussler,
and Gerstmann who meant to tile
our temporal roofs with amyloid.
Epitope CT-II is void
and awaiting trial.

All have been taken except for
the spymaster and his receptor
who successfully fled the secretariat

into the heart of the Down's.

There they may be counted on to wreak havoc
on heavily silvered neuronal circuits
fifty years sooner than before. Nothing
in cleavage is worse than a peavish
enzyme gone bad like this one, a sheep
fanged in wolf's clothing!


III. The Conspirator's Version

We have been betrayed. PreA4s
are taken from their ectodomains
in peptide chains.

Called traitors and sabateurs,
by scientific provocateurs,
tieless, beltless,
under argyrophilic bulbs
they have been coerced
into giving more than their names.

The prions are all in prison
except for our preceptor
quietly living so long
at 21q21
Alzheimer Lane. He has gone
underground to carry on
the struggle in the Down's.


IV. The Iowa Writer's Workshop Version

How beautifully knowledge increments, how
    easily we learn
from blot analysis and the numbering scheme of
    Kang

that we will fade, that cleavage of an epitope
can mislay in amyloid all of the laughter, love and
    hope

which might justify us if not mislaid, that links
    between
unlike diseases of the old and young, unfelt,
    unseen,

remove the soul's delight. It makes us braver,
    knowing
how fragile we are, how ripe for overthrowing.


V. The Enzyme's Version

Comrade, in cleaving PreA4 I mean
no harm. Our needs are complementary.
The wisest parasite will always see
host needs met first, a good marine
will not despise the swabbie's point of view.
It is as much my purpose to avoid
laying neuronal tiles of amyloid
as it is yours to catch me if I do.

Something other than this epitope
we share a need for, causes the disease
you fear so much. Surely we can hope
that if we live with nothing in excess
as ancient Greece advised, the two of us
can shame our common gene to know itself.


VI. The Principal Investigator's Version

Having a mind so avid for recognition that
    I spent
half my lifetime preparing for this moment, I take
    pride
in having discovered the antibody specific and
    sensitive to epitope CT-II of PreA4.
It's important work; it will help the half dozen
    other investigators who know
what I'm talking about. I can also be proud of the
managerial skill with which this paper of many
    authors

was put together. Not one grammatical flaw or
    factual error,
and it was published in the most respected venue
    of them all,
*New England Journal of Medicine*, which
reporters always read for their leads. So do deans.
    The paper is good

for a full professorship at least, perhaps an
    invitation
to be considered for an empty chair. But looking
    back
I sometimes wonder if I wouldn't have been
    happier
writing music that no one listens to.
Rumble is sometimes odd.
He says that we exercised our minds so much
    discovering
facts about Alzheimer's amyloidosis we have
immunized ourselves against getting it. It's one
of his better ideas. I've created a logic-tight
compartment for it. It comforts. it's not like
    truth.

                              *Morton Pollycove*

## Smoking

I like the cool and heft of it, dull metal on the palm,
And the click, the hiss, the spark fuming into flame,
Boldface of fire, the rage and sway of it, raw blue at th
    base
And a slope of gold, a touch to the packed tobacco, the tip
Turned red as a warning light, blown brighter by the
    breath,
The pull and the pump of it, and the paper's white
Smoothed now to ash as the smoke draws back, drawn down
To the black crust of lungs, tar and poisons in the pink,
And the blood sorting it out, veins tight and the heart
    slow,
The push and wheeze of it, a sweep of plumes in the air
Like a shako of horses dragging a hearse through the late
    centennium,
London, at the end of December, in the dark and fog.

*Elton Glaser*

## The Common Cold

Go hang yourself, you old M.D.!
You shall no longer sneer at me.
Pick up your hat and stethoscope,
Go wash your mouth with laundry soap;
I contemplate a joy exquisite
In never paying you for your visit.
I did not call you to be told
My malady is a common cold.

By pounding brow and swollen lip;
By fever's hot and scaly grip;
By these two red redundant eyes
That weep like woeful April skies;
By racking snuffle, snort, and sniff;
By handkerchief after handkerchief;
This cold you wave away as naught
Is the damnedest cold man ever caught.

Give ear, you scientific fossil!
Here is the genuine Cold Colossal;
The Cold of which researchers dream,
The Perfect Cold, the Cold Supreme.
This honored system humbly holds
The Super-cold to end all colds;
The Cold Crusading far Democracy;
The Führer of the Streptococcracy.

Bacilli swarm within my portals
Such as were ne'er conceived by mortals,
But bred by scientists wise and hoary
In some Olympian laboratory;
Bacteria as large as mice,
With feet of fire and heads of ice
Who never interrupt for slumber
Their stamping elephantine rumba.

A common cold, forsooth, gadzooks!
Then Venus showed promise of good looks;
Don Juan was a budding gallant,

And Shakespeare's plays show signs of talent;
The Arctic winter is rather coolish,
And your diagnosis is fairly foolish.
Oh what derision history holds
For the man who belittled the Cold of Colds!

*Ogden Nash*

## A Meeting on Quality Assurance

What makes me sit here when I could choose
Delivery
From this great desert site?
Ideas dry as dunes stretch clear to lunch.
Jargon dries my brain.
A sandstorm stings my eyes.
If I were not professional
(Deducting my expenses)
I might stretch hugely now
And walk out
Into life.

*George Bascom*

## The Pathologist

In the laboratory despite the late
Hour, the pathologist is still up
Testing his colonies. His searching loop
Has ruffled many a paling agar plate.

One dish alone is still suffused with blood:
Here grows the germ of suffering — a rare strain
Has shaped its lair like a medusa mane.
The poisonous spores keep breeding vicious brood.

The worn pathologist, still curious, drops
His latest serum on the matted growth —
A furious spasm shakes the quiet house.

A dying shiver — then the writhing stops.
The master with a smile turns out the light
And hides the wonder serum out of sight.

*Henry Shore*

## The X-Ray Waiting Room in the Hospital

I am dressed in my big shoes and wrinkled socks
And one of the light blue, much-laundered smocks
The men and women of this country wear.
All of us miss our own underwear
And the old days. These new, plain, mean
Days of pain and care, this routine
Misery has made us into cases, the one case
The one doctor cures forever. . . The face
The patients have in common hopes without hope
For something from outside the machine—its wife,
Its husband—to burst in and hand it life;
But when the door opens, it's another smock.
It looks at us, we look at it. Our little flock
Of blue-smocked sufferers, in naked equality,
Longs for each nurse and doctor who goes by
Well and dressed, to make friends with, single out, the *I*
That used to be, but we are indistinguishable.
It is better to lie flat upon a table,
A dye in my spine. The roentgenologist
Introduces me to a kind man, a specialist
In spines like mine: the lights go out, he rotates me.
My myelogram is negative. This elates me,
The good-humored specialist congratulates me,
And I take off my smock in joy, put on
My own pajamas, my own dressing gown,
And ride back to my own room, 601.

*Randall Jarrell*

## The Germ

A mighty creature is the germ,
Though smaller than the pachyderm.
His customary dwelling place
Is deep within the human race.
His childish pride he often pleases
By giving people strange diseases.
Do you, my poppet, feel infirm?
You probably contain a germ.

*Ogden Nash*

## Silas Gill

*Osteoarthritic Cervical Spurring*

This time they found you on the street
Bawling that you couldn't walk,
A sixty-eight year old, white-haired baby.
They'd heard that before, but never in the summer
When street sleeping was good.
So they threw you, your bottle and your tears
In the paddy.

"Doc, we were gonna keep him in a cell
But thought you aughta take a look."
Knowing the sergeant's habits
I knew this to mean that you were
Making too much noise in jail.

You had very good reason to bawl.
Three plus knee jerks and wasted quads;
From the films of your neck it was hard to see
How anything could pass from your skull to your legs,
And we transferred you to neurosurgery.

In a short three weeks after cutting
You walked off the ward with a limp,
Twirling your cane.
I returned your wink and knew
That when I saw you next winter
I'd listen with care to every one
Of your noisy complaints.

*K. D. Beernink*

## On Living

I

Living is no laughing matter:
             you must live with great seriousness
                     like a squirrel, for example—
  I mean without looking for something beyond and above living,
                        I mean living must be your whole occupation.
Living is no laughing matter:
             you must take it seriously,
           so much so and to such a degree
  that, for example, your hands tied behind your back,
                   your back to the wall,
  or else in a laboratory
             in your white coat and safety glasses,
             you can die for people—
  even for people whose faces you've never seen,
  even though you know living
             is the most real, the most beautiful thing.
I mean, you must take living so seriously
   that even at seventy, for example, you'll plant olive trees—
   and not for your children, either,
   but because although you fear death you don't believe it,
   because living, I mean, weighs heavier.

II

Let's say we're seriously ill, need surgery—
which is to say we might not get up
                     from the white table.
Even though it's impossible not to feel sad
                   about going a little too soon,
we'll still laugh at the jokes being told,
we'll look out the window to see if it's raining,
or still wait anxiously
            for the latest newscast…

Let's say we're at the front—
        for something worth fighting for, say.
There, in the first offensive, on that very day,
        we might fall on our face, dead.
We'll know this with a curious anger,
        but we'll still worry ourselves to death
        about the outcome of the war, which could last years.
Let's say we're In prison
and close to fifty,
and we have eighteen more years, say,
        before the iron doors will open.
We'll still live with the outside,
with its people and animals, struggle and wind—
        I mean with the outside beyond the walls.
I mean, however and wherever we are,
        we must live as if we will never die.

III

This earth will grow cold,
a star among stars
        and one of the smallest,
a gilded mote on blue velvet—
        I mean *this,* our great earth.
This earth will grow cold one day,
not like a block of ice
or a dead cloud even
but like an empty walnut it will roll along
        in pitch-black space...
You must grieve for this right now
—you have to feel this sorrow now—
for the world must be loved this much
        if you're going to say "I lived"...

*Nazim Hikmet*
(translated by Mutlu Konuk and Randy Blasing)

## On the Subject
## of Doctors

I like to see doctors cough.
What kind of human being
would grab all your money
just when you're down?
I'm not saying they enjoy this:
"Sorry, Mr. Rodriguez, that's it,
no hope! You might as well
hand over your wallet." Hell no,
they'd rather be playing golf
and swapping jokes about our feet.

Some of them smoke marijuana
and are alcoholics, and their moral
turpitude is famous: who gets to see
most sex organs in the world? Not
poets. With the hours they keep
they need drugs more than anyone.
Germ city, there's no hope
looking down those fire-engine throats.
They're bound to get sick themselves
sometime; and I happen to be there
myself in a high fever
taking my plastic medicine seriously
with the doctors, who are dying.

*James Tate*

## Upon a Physitian

THou cam'st to cure me (Doctor) of my cold,
And caught'st thy selfe the more by twenty fold:
Prethee goe home; and for thy credit be
First cur'd thy selfe;[1] then come and cure me.

*Robert Herrick*

[1] Luke iv.23, "Physician, heal thyself:"

## Skin

Obedient daily dress,
You cannot always keep
That unfakable young surface.
You must learn your lines—
Anger, amusement, sleep;
Those few forbidding signs

Of the continuous coarse
Sand-laden wind, time;
You must thicken, work loose
Into an old bag
Carrying a soiled name.
Parch then; be roughened; sag;

And pardon me, that I
Could find, when you were new,
No brash festivity
To wear you at, such as
Clothes are entitled to
Till the fashion changes.

*Philip Larkin*

## Departmental Function

It was a faculty affair
all intelligence and wit
sherry balancing
on slender stemmed bon mots
laughter rising like the fragrance
of rare flowers
and everywhere horn rims clashing
like the crash of antlered elk.

*George Bascom*

## The Doctor Sighs

as he removes the otoscope.
"It's not just the hammer,
anvil, and stirrup," he says.
"It's the blacksmith, too.
And the dry goods store
with the weaselly clerk,
not to mention the saloon
rife with cowboys and
a prostitute with humble
cleavage. And I'm afraid
it's also the calibrated hearts
in that freezing ten-room
hotel, the mayor's daughter
weeping into well water,
the moon spreading its
anxious light over everything.

In short, Ronald, I'm not
Surprised you called
for an appointment today."

*Ron Koertge*

## Tree of Knowledge

If you know the name of the poem you would like to hear,
Press one, now.
To search the index for a poem or poet,
Press two, now.
For critical assessment of a poem,
Press three, now.
To speak with a poet, hold the line
Or press zero at any time.

The poem you have selected,
"Stopping by Woods on a Snowy Evening,"
Is currently in use. Please select another.
The poem you have selected,
"To Autumn," is currently in use.
Please select another.
The poem you have selected,
"Because I Could Not Stop for Death,"
Is no longer in service.
Please hold the line for critical assessment.

For definitions of kindness, press one, now.
To hear other reasons why Death stops,
Press two, now. If you feel as though
The top of your head has physically been taken off,
Press three, now. For other poems about Death,
Or for Death's current itinerary,
Hold the line and a poet will answer.

For "Thirteen Ways of Looking at a Blackbird,"
Press one, now.
If the mind of the tree and the mind of the bird are one,
Press two at any time.
To have a mind of winter,
Press three, now.
For ideas about the thing,
Press four, now.
For the thing itself, or to compose your own poem,
Please hold the line.

For the word, "heart," press one, now.
For the word, "tears," press two, now.
For the words, "Eye," "Cheek," "Lip," or "Brow,"
Search for Donne. When thou hast done,
Press three to return to the main menu.

The word "heart" is currently in use. Please select another.
The word "beating" is currently in use. Please select another.

The word "twittering" is no longer is service.
For help in choosing between two roads,
Please hold the line and a poet will answer.
To make it new, press pound.

For God's sake hold your tongue and let me love,
Press one, now.
If you can keep your head while those around you,
Press two, now.
To three posts driven upright in the ground,
Press three, now.
To reap a time to sow,
Please hold the line and a poet will ask you
If you know the name of the poem you would like to hear.

*Daniel Bosch*

# Biographical Sketches

**Abse, Dannie.**
(b. 1923) A native of Wales, born in Cardiff, Abse became a physician in 1950, two years after the publication of his first book of poetry, *After Every Green Thing*. He has continued both vocations, practicing as a chest medicine specialist and writing about his medical and personal experiences. Abse has published numerous collections of poetry, including *Running Late* (2006). He also writes fiction, plays, and nonfiction.

**Agodon, Kelli Russell.**
(b. 1971) Born and raised in Seattle, Agodon has published two books of poetry, *Geography* (2003) and *Small Knots* (2004). She continues to live in Washington, where she has been working on peace-related issues via *The Making of Peace: Broadside Series* and is now editing an anthology on mother-hood. Agodon's poems have been featured in many magazines and journals, including the *Atlantic Monthly* and *Prairie Schooner*.

**Akhmatova, Anna.**
(1889-1966) Born in Odessa, Ukraine, Akhmatova (pseudonym of Anna Andreevna Gorenko) began writing poetry at an early age and became a leader in the Acmeist school of Russian poetry. Her works, banned by the government for many years, included an elegy for the prisoners of Stalin, "Requiem." Today, she is considered one of Russia's preeminent poets.

**Akiko, Yosano.**
(1878-1942) Yosano Akiko was the pen name of Yosano Shiyo, a feminist, pacifist, and one of Japan's most famous and controversial post-classical female poets. An important contributor to the poetry magazine *Myojo*, her first volume of tanka was *Midaregami* (1901). She published over 20 works, including an autobiography. Her poem "Thou Shalt Not Die" became a song as a form of anti-war protest. Akiko died of a stroke.

**Angelou, Maya.**
(b. 1928) Born in St. Louis, Missouri, Angelou is a prolific writer of both poetry and prose. In 1993 she recited her poem "On the Pulse of Morning" at the inauguration of President Clinton. An educa-tor, historian, actress and playwright, as well as a poet, Angelou has taught American Studies at Wake Forest University since 1981.

**Appleman, Philip.**
(b. 1926) Born in Kendallville, Indiana, Appleman is Distinguished Professor Emeritus at Indiana University, Bloomington. He has published seven books of poetry, including *New and Selected Poems, 1956-1996* (University of Arkansas Press), and three novels. Some of his writings are inspired by the works of Charles Darwin.

**Auden, W. H.**
(1907-1973) Wystan Hugh Auden was born in York. He emigrated from England to America in 1939, eventually becoming an American citizen. In 1948 he won the Pulitzer Prize for his long poem, *The Age of Anxiety.*

**Barnstone, Willis.**
(b. 1927) Barnstone, born in Lewiston, Maine, is Distinguished Professor Emeritus at Indiana University. He has taught internationally and written and translated extensively. Recently, he has been working on a translation of the New Testament from the Greek. His works include more than a dozen books of poetry, including *Alphabet of the Night: New and Selected Poems, 1948-1998* (1999).

**Bascom, George.**
(1921-1995) Bascom wrote five volumes of poetry from 1982 through 1993, all published by Sunflower University Press. His poems cover a wide range of topics in a variety of forms, ranging from free verse to the sonnet. Many examine his medical experiences, both as physician and patient. He died of prostate cancer after having practiced surgery in Manhattan, Kansas, for over 35 years.

**Bashō, Matsuo.**
(ca. 1644-1694) Bashō achieved prominence in the early years of the Tokugawa shogunate in early modern Japan. Possibly the son of a samurai, he rejected a military life to wander, teach, and write. Eza Pound and the Imagists, and later the poets of the Beat generation, cited Bashō as a major influence. Today, for many, his name is synonymous with the haiku form.

**Battles, William Snowden.**
(1827-1895?) Battles was born near Philadelphia, received his medical degree in 1852, and practiced medicine in Ohio. In addition to his poetry, he published widely in the medical literature.

**Beaumont, Jeanne Marie.**
(b. 1954) Beaumont grew up in the Philadelphia area and has taught extensively. Her first book, *Placebo Effects,* was published in 1997. Her poems have appeared in many anthologies and journals. *Afraid So* was made into a short film by Jay Rosenblatt and was shown at international film festivals in 2006.

**Beernink, K. D.**
(1938-1969) A year after receiving his medical degree from Stanford, Beernink developed chronic myelocytic leukemia. He worked as a research fellow at Stanford and founded a local chapter of Physicians for Social Responsibility. During his illness, he wrote poetry as doctor/patient, experiencing many of the emotions of his patients.

**Berlin, Richard M.**
(b. 1950) Born in Jersey City, New Jersey, Berlin is a psychiatrist whose poems reflect his experiences as student/doctor/healer. Although he did not begin writing poetry until in his 40's, his poems have already garnered awards: *How JFK Killed My Father* won the 2002 Pearl Poetry Prize. Berlin teaches psychiatry at the University of Massachusetts Medical School.

**Berry, Wendell.**
(b. 1934) Berry writes poetry, essays, short stories, and novels, with over 30 books to his credit. Among his titles are *Traveling at Home* (1989), *There is Singing Around Me* (1976), and *Window Poems* (2007). Berry has taught widely and lives on a farm in Kentucky, the state of his birth.

**Bly, Robert.**
(b. 1926) Bly was born in Madison, Minnesota. An influential figure in American letters, he has written more than 30 books of poetry and has been editor of *The Sixties* magazine. He paid tribute to fellow poet William Stafford, several of whose poems appear in this anthology, in the poem "When William Stafford Died." Bly lives in Minnesota.

**Booth, Philip.**
(1925-2007) Booth was born in Hanover, New Hampshire, and spent much of his early years in coastal Maine. Booth studied with Robert Frost at Dartmouth College, where he later taught for a year. He produced ten books of poetry, including his first, *Letters from a Distant Land* (1957), and *Lifelines: Selected Poems, 1950-1999* (1999).

**Bosch, Daniel.**
Daniel Bosch has been a preceptor in expository writing at Harvard University, a former poetry editor of *Harvard Review,* and an editor of "Negative Images" at PoetryNet. His poems have appeared in *Agni, The Literary Review, The New Republic,* and other magazines. In 1998, he won *Boston Review's* first annual poetry contest. Bosch lives in Boston.

**Browning, Elizabeth Barrett.**
(1806-1861) Browning's poetical reputation, like that of her husband Robert and other Victorian poets, has vacillated. Born in Durham, she lived in Italy with her spouse for almost all of their married life. Some of her poems focus on social issues such as child labor and political freedom. She remains best known, however, for her love poems, *Sonnets from the Portuguese.*

**Bryant, William Cullen.**
(1794-1878) Considered by some to be the father of American poetry, Bryant was a lawyer, editor, biographer, and an influential figure politically, socially, and in the arts. He was born in Cummington, Massachusetts, and spent much of his life in New York City, where he was editor, then an owner of, the *Evening Post.* Among Bryant's better known poems are "Thanatopsis" and "To a Waterfowl."

**Bunford, Jan.**
(b. 1957) Born in Rumford, Maine, Bunford works as an administrator at the University of Maine in Augusta. She writes poems and essays touching on her personal and family experiences and the natural world, as well as on social issues. "One Jar, Two Sticks" was published in *The Maine Scholar.* In 2001, Bunford was co-recipient of the Richard Carbonneau Poetry Prize.

**Burns, Ralph.**
(b. 1949) Born in Norman, Oklahoma, Burns has published six collections of poems. He is a winner of the Field Poetry Prize, the Iowa Poetry Prize, and two fellowships from the NEA.

**Campo, Rafael.**
(b. 1964) Campo was born in Dover, New Jersey. His first book of poetry, *The Other Man Was Me: A Voyage to the New World*, was published after his graduation from Harvard Medical School, where he now practices medicine. In a *Salon* article, Campo articulated his belief that poetry and its organic rhythms can heal, and he incorporates poetry into his treatment of patients. Campo's prose includes *The Healing Art: A Doctor's Black Bag of Poetry.*

**Carver, Raymond.**
(1938-1988) Born in Clatskanie, Oregon, Carver is known widely for his short stories. Carver suffered from lung cancer and his illness and treatment influenced some of his writing. "Late Fragment" appeared in his last book, *In a Marine Light: Selected Poems,* published the year of his death.

**Cavafy, Constantine P.**
(1863-1933) Cavafy was born of Greek heritage in Alexandria, Egypt, and lived there most of his life, working as a civil servant. He did not come to be recognized as a major poet until years after his death from cancer in 1933. Since then, his poetry has been translated widely. "Ithaka" is perhaps his best-known poem.

**Cleary, Suzanne.**
Suzanne Cleary's books include *Keeping Time* (2002) and *Trick Pear* (2007), both published by Carnegie-Mellon University Press, and a chapbook, *Blue Cloth*. A professor at SUNY Rockland, she has been involved with the Frost Place, a nonprofit educational center for poetry and the arts based at Robert Frost's old homestead in Franconia, New Hampshire.

**Clifton, Lucille.**
(b. 1936) Two years after publishing her first collection of poems, Clifton gave up working as a government employee to become a writer in residence at Coppin State University in Maryland. A former Poet Laureate for Maryland, Clifton has written ten volumes of poetry and many children's books. Clifton was born in Depew, New York.

**Coleman, Wanda.**
(b. 1946) Coleman's extensive oeuvre includes poetry, stories, essays, creative non-fiction and a novel. She was the 1999 recipient of the Lenore Marshall Poetry Prize. *Jazz and Twelve O'Clock Tales* was published in 2007. Los Angeles-based Coleman frequently performs her poetry, subjects of which include race and class, politics and art. She has been a journalist, waitress, and medical secretary.

**Collins, Billy.**
(b. 1941) Collins was born in New York City. He has received numerous fellowships and honors as a poet, including being named US Poet Laureate in 2001 and receiving the 2004 Mark Twain Award for humorous poetry. His *Nine Horses* (2002) was a national bestseller; *The Trouble with Poetry and Other Poems* was published in 2005. He has taught at a variety of colleges and universities.

**Coulehan, Jack.**
(b. 1943) A medical doctor and prize-winning poet, Coulehan has written four volumes of poetry, including *Medicine Stone* (2002). He is co-editor with Angela Belli of two anthologies of poems written by physicians, *Primary Care* and *Blood and Bone*. Coulehan worked on the Navajo Reservation before teaching at SUNY Stony Brook until his retirement in 2007. In addition to poetry, Coulehan has written books on medical ethics and practice.

**Cowper, Williams.**
(1731-1800) English poet and hymnodist. Popular during his lifetime, Cowper wrote of everyday people's lives in the English country side. His deep sympathy with nature, and love of animal life, were to influencec much later English poetry. Cowper's translation of Homer's *Iliad* and *Odyssey* was published in 1791.

**Cummings, E. E.**
(1894-1962) Edward Estlin Cummings was born in Cambridge, Massachusetts, and attended Harvard University, where he first published his poems. He is best-known for his idiosyncratic style, which challenges the rules of grammar in punctuation and structure. Cummings was also a playwright. At the time of his death, he was one of the most widely read poets in the United States.

**Davie, Donald.**
(1922-1995) Davie was born in Barnsley, Yorkshire, England, and taught at the University of Essex and later in America. Many of his works, including poems and criticism, have been published by Carcanet Press.

**Delanty, Greg.**
(b. 1958) Delanty, born in Ireland, is now an American citizen . He teaches at St. Michael's College, Vermont. His five volumes of poetry include *Cast in the Fire* and *The Hellbox*. His *Collected Poems* appeared in 2006.

**Dickinson, Emily.**
(1830-1886) Dickinson was born and died in Amherst, Massachusetts. Few of her poems were published during her lifetime. However, after her death her sister discovered her vast amount of poetry which, despite her reclusive life, encompassed insightful observations on life and nature.

**Dickinson, Josephine.**
(b. 1957) Dickinson was born and raised in South London. After a childhood illness, she became profoundly deaf at the age of six. She read Classics at Oxford, has taught and composed music, and made her American debut with the collection *Silence Fell* in 2007.

**Djanikian, Gregory.**
(b. 1949) Born in Alexandria, Djanikian moved at the age of six with his family to Pennsylvania, where he now lives. From his first collection, *The Man in the Middle* (1984), to his fifth, *So I Will Till the Ground* (2006), Djanikian has received many awards for his poetry. He has been professor of English at the University of Pennsylvania since 1983.

**Donne, John.**
(1572-1631) Born in London, Donne is perhaps the best-known of the "metaphysical poets." His work, which includes both religious and non-religious verse, widely influenced 20th-century poets. His major works include *Songs* and *Holy Sonnets*.

**Dove, Rita.**
(b. 1952) Dove was born in Akron, Ohio. Her collection of poems, *Thomas and Beulah,* won the Pulitzer Prize in 1987. She served as US Poet Laureate from 1993 to 1995 and was one of three Special Bicentennial Consultants from 1999 to 2000. She is professor of English at the University of Virginia. In addition to her verse, Dove has written short stories and a novel, *Through the Ivory Gate.*

**Ellis, Havelock.**
(1859-1940) Born in Surrey, Ellis was a physician and poet. Criticized for being an ardent proponent of sex education, Ellis wrote many books and essays on the subject, as well as on psychiatry. Some of his writings were banned in England. Ellis was acquainted with H. G. Wells and George Bernard Shaw.

**Fallon, John.**
(b. 1901?) Fallon, of Worcester, Massachusetts, was a surgeon, a collector of medical literature, poet, and author of numerous medical articles.

**Flenniken, Kathleen.**
Before becoming a poet, Flenniken worked as a civil engineer, including three years at the Hanford Nuclear Reservation—the subject of some of her recent poems. Her first collection of poetry, *Famous* (2005), won the *Prairie Schooner* Prize for Poetry. Flenniken lives in Seattle and is co-editor and president of Floating Bridge Press, a nonprofit organization that publishes Washington State poets.

**Fumiko, Nakaj.**
(1922-1954)  Born in Obihiro, Hokkaido, Japan, Fumiko began writing tanka more seriously after a failed marriage. Her first poems were published in small magazines in 1946. In 1952, she was diagnosed with breast cancer. She died two years later, the same year she won acclaim after winning a national tanka contest. Her last book appeared posthumously.

**Glaser, Elton.**
A native of New Orleans, Glaser has spent much of his time in Ohio, teaching and writing. He has composed over 500 poems, many of which have appeared in anthologies and magazines. He has been the recipient of numerous fellowships and poetry prizes. His collection *Pelican Tracks* appeared in 2003.

**Glück, Louise.**
(b. 1943)  Glück was born in New York City. She won the Pulitzer Prize for Poetry in 1993 for her collection *The Wild Iris*. Other titles include *The House on Marshland* and *Meadowlands*. Glück served as Special Bicentennial Consultant to the Library of Congress in 2000 and was Poet Laureate from 2003 to 2004.

**Gunn, Thom.**
(1929-2004)  Born in Kent, Gunn served two years in the British National Service before attending Trinity College. His first collection, *Fighting Terms,* appeared in 1950. He later moved to San Francisco and over the next several decades wrote many volumes of poetry, notably, in 1992, *The Man with Night Sweats*, a tribute to friends who had contracted AIDS, which won him the Lenore Marshall Poetry Prize. Gunn died in San Francisco.

**Hardy, Thomas.**
(1840-1928)  Born in Dorsetshire, Hardy was an architect before turning to writing. He became famous as a novelist (e.g., *Far from the Madding Crowd, The Mayor of Casterbridge, Tess of the D'Urbervilles*) but, after the controversial reception of *Jude the Obscure,* he abandoned fiction for poetry. He wrote a long poem about the Napoleonic wars (*The Dynasts*) and many lyrics.

**Heaney, Seamus.**
(b. 1939)  Born in County Derry, Northern Ireland, Heaney was a lecturer at St. Joseph's College in Belfast, where he met Derek Mahon, and later professor of poetry at Oxford. In 1995 he was awarded the Nobel Prize in Literature. Heaney now resides in Dublin, spending part of the year teaching at Harvard University. His body of work includes *Opened Ground* (1992), *The Spirit Level* (1996), and an acclaimed translation of *Beowulf* (2000).

**Heatter, Virginia M.**
Heatter lives in Nashua, New Hampshire. She is co-founder of *The New Hampshire Review*, a biannual on-line publication.

**Henley, William Ernest.**
(1849-1903)  A Victorian poet, Henley was born in Gloucester. He was afflicted at the age of 12 with tuberculosis of the bone. During a later hospitalization he began writing "In Hospital." He wrote four plays with his friend Robert Louis Stevenson but is best known for his poem "Invictus."

**Herrick, Robert.**
(1591-1674) An English poet who was influenced by classical Roman poetry, Herrick often took English country life as his subject. He was ordained a priest in 1623. Considered the greatest Cavalier poet, Herrick wrote some 1300 poems, most of which appeared in *Hesperides* (1648).

**Hewitt, John.**
(1907-1987) Hewitt was born and lived predominantly in Northern Ireland. He wrote poetry for several decades and had a keen interest and involvement in politics. He wrote numerous collections of poetry, many published by Blackstaff Press.

**Hikmet, Nazim.**
(1902-1963) Hikmet was born in Selânik (now Thessaloniki, Greece), the westernmost metropolis of the Ottoman Empire, and was raised in Istanbul. He left occupied Turkey after World War I, attending university in Moscow. For the next several decades, Hikmet spent his life between Turkey and Russia, at one point being imprisoned in Turkey for his political writings and escaping to Russia. He is now widely regarded as the first modern Turkish poet.

**Hoagland, Tony.**
(b. 1953) Hoagland was born in Fort Bragg, North Carolina. His works, which have received many poetry prizes, include *Sweet Ruin* (1992), *What Narcissism Means to Me* (2003), and *Hard Rain* (2005). Hoagland teaches at the University of Houston and Warren Wilson College.

**Holder, Elmo.**
(1937-1975) Holder was born in Texas but lived mostly in Indiana and New York City. His *Regions and Other Poems* was published by Whippoorwill Publications (Evansville).

**Holub, Miroslav.**
(1923-1998) A Czech immunologist, born in Plzen, Holub wrote scientific papers as well as poetry. His writings were banned in Czechoslovakia for nearly a decade during Communist rule. His works have been widely translated; collections include *Intensive Care: Selected and New Poems* (1996) and *Poems Before & After: Collected English Translations* (new edition 2007).

**Ignatow, David.**
(1914-1997) Ignatow was born in Brooklyn and spent most of his life in the New York area. He published more than 20 books of verse between 1943 and 1999. Ignatow taught at several universities and colleges, including the New School for Social Research, the University of Kentucky, and Columbia University, and received many honors over his career.

**Jarrell, Randall.**
(1914-1965) A native of Nashville, Jarrell was an important literary critic as well as a poet. He studied with Robert Penn Warren and worked with Robert Lowell. He joined the army in 1942 and wrote about soldiers and war. In his role as critic he helped establish the reputation of William Carlos Williams. Jarrell was consultant to the Library of Congress from 1956 to 1958. His last volume was *The Lost World* (1965).

**Jenkins, Louis.**
Jenkins lives in Minnesota and has written several collections of poetry, including *The Winter Road*, *Just Above Water*, and *Nice Fish: New and Selected Prose Poems*, all from Holy Cow! Press. *All Tangled Up with the Living* and *An Almost Human Gesture* are available from Ally Press Center.

**Jones, Alice.**
(b. 1949) A physician specializing in internal medicine and psychiatry, Jones now practices psycho-analysis in California and is co-editor of Apogee Press. Her poems have appeared in *Ploughshares* and *The Harvard Review*, among other magazines. Her award-winning books include *The Knot* and *Isthmus* (Alice James Books).

**Kelly-DeWitt, Susan.**
Kelly-DeWitt lives in California. Her works include the collection *The Fortunate Islands*, the forth-coming *Ghostfire*, as well as several chapbooks. Her poems have been included in anthologies and in literary journals such as *Prairie Schooner* and *Spoon River Quarterly*. She teaches at Sacramento City College and the University of California, Davis.

**Kenyon, Jane.**
(1847-1995) Kenyon was born in Ann Arbor, Michigan, and grew up in the Midwest. She later moved to New Hampshire with her writer husband Donald Hall. She wrote five volumes of poetry as well as notable translations of the poems of Anna Akhmatova. She was Poet Laureate of New Hampshire at the time of her death from leukemia.

**Kinnell, Galway.**
(b. 1927) Born in Providence, Rhode Island, Kinnell was a classmate of W. S. Merwin at Princeton. He has published several volumes of poetry and is the winner of numerous poetry prizes and a MacArthur Fellowship. He was Erich Maria Remarque Professor of Creative Writing at NYU until his retirement in 2005.

**Knight, Etheridge.**
(1931-1991) A native of Corinth, Mississippi, Knight had an early interest in improvised poetry and storytelling. He was wounded during service in the army in Korea. While imprisoned for several years, Knight began writing poetry, much of it about that experience. His first book, *Poems from Prison* (1968), was published a year before his release; he later edited *Black Voices from Prison*. Knight received his bachelor's degree in American poetry and criminal justice in 1990.

**Koch, Kenneth.**
(1925-2002) Born in Cincinnati, Koch moved to New York City and was associated with the New York School of poetry, a break with confessional poetry that drew inspiration from contemporary artists such as Jackson Pollack and various European painters. He wrote many books of poetry, from *Poems* in 1953 to *New Addresses* in 2000, and received several awards. Koch also wrote short plays and was professor of English at Columbia University.

**Koertge, Ron.**
Koertge lives in South Pasadena, California, and taught English for many years at Pasadena City College. His books include *Dairy Cows* and *Making Love to Roget's Wife* (University of Arkansas Press). In addition to poetry, Koertge has written many young adult novels. Humor is integral to his writing.

**Kooser, Ted.**
(b. 1939) Born in Ames, Iowa, Kooser has written a dozen collections of poetry and has received numerous literary awards. He was US Poet Laureate from 2004-2006. Kooser now lives in Nebraska and is a professor at the University of Nebraska at Lincoln. His most recent work is *Flying at Night* (2005).

**Larkin, Philip.**
(1922-1985) Poet, novelist, and jazz critic, Philip Larkin was born in Coventry and spent much of his career as University Librarian at the University of Hull. In 1955, his second collection of poems, *The Less Deceived*, established him as a major voice in contemporary English letters. Two more collections solidified both his popularity and critical reputation, and he was offered the Poet Laureateship of England in 1984 but declined the post. In 2003, Larkin was named best-loved British poet of the last 50 years in a survey of the members of the Poetry Book Society.

**Lowry, Malcolm.**
(1909-1957) An English poet and novelist, Lowry was born in Cheshire County. His turbulent personal life was marked by travels to mainland Europe, the United States, Mexico, and Canada. His novel *Under the Volcano* (1947) is considered a modern masterpiece. A documentary, *Volcano: An Inquiry into the Life and Death of Malcolm Lowry* (1976), depicts Lowry's life and "death by misadventure."

**Lurie, Bobbi.**
Lurie's poems have been published in *The American Poetry Review* and other magazines. She lives in New Mexico. Her second collection of poetry is *Letter from the Lawn* (2006).

**Lux, Thomas.**
(b. 1946) Lux was born in Northampton, Massachusetts. He has taught at universities across the United States and has nearly 20 published works, including *The Cradle Place* (2004), *The Street of Clocks* (2001), and *The Land Sighted* (1970).

**Mahon, Derek.**
(b. 1941) Born in Belfast, Mahon has written many collections of poetry including *In Their Element: A Selection of Poems* (1977) with Seamus Heaney. He is the recipient of a Guggenheim Fellowship and has received other honors.

**Masson, Veneta.**
Masson is a registered nurse, poet, and essayist who lives in Washington, D.C. She has written two books based on her experiences as an inner-city nurse: one, *Rehab at the Florida Avenue Grill*, a volume of poetry; the other, *Ninth Street Notebook: Voice of a Nurse in the City*, stories and prose. Masson was one of the co-founders of Community Medical Care, a clinic in inner-city Washington, D.C.

**Mehta, Diane.**
Mehta lives in Brooklyn. She is a poet and critic whose writing has appeared in *Prairie Schooner, The Southern Review,* and other magazines. Mehta's books include *The Four Seasons, Arranged Marriage,* and *Hot December: Memory of Holiday in Bombay.*

**Merton, Thomas.**
(1915-1968) Born in France, Merton graduated from Columbia University with a degree in English. He later became intensely interested in theology and Catholicism and was ordained in 1949, eventually entering the Trappist order at the Abbey of Our Lady of Gethsemani in Kentucky. A prolific writer of both poetry and prose and author of over 60 books, he was a fervent believer in nonviolence and a proponent of inter-religious dialogue.

**Millay, Edna St. Vincent.**
(1892-1950) A modern master of the sonnet, Millay was born in Rockland, Maine. She won the Pulitzer Prize for *The Harp Weaver and Other Poems* (1923), her fourth collection. "Vincent," as she was called, also wrote three plays in verse and a libretto for the opera *The King's Henchman.*

**Milosz, Czeslaw.**
(1911-2004) Milosz was born in Seteiniai, Lithuania. His poetry was first published in the 1930s. During the Second World War, he worked for underground presses in Warsaw. Milosz moved to France in the early 1950s, and in 1960 came to the United States. He taught at the University of California, Berkeley, for several decades. In 1980 he was awarded the Nobel Prize in Literature.

**Mueller, Lisel.**
(b. 1924) Born in Hamburg, Germany, Mueller and her family fled to the United States in 1939. She has published eight books of poetry and received the Pulitzer Prize in 1997 for *Alive Together: New & Selected Poems* (1996). She has been a visiting writer at the University of Chicago and Washington University, St. Louis. Mueller lives in Lake Forest, Illinois.

**Nash, Ogden.**
(1902-1971) One of America's best known and oft-quoted poets, Nash wrote light verse characterized by humor and wit. Nash was born in Rye, New York, and published his first collection in 1931 (*Hard Lines*). He worked for many years at the Doubleday, Doran publishing house. A popular speaker and lecturer, Nash also wrote the lyrics for the musical comedy *One Touch of Venus* (1943). A postage stamp honoring Nash was issued in 2002.

**Nashe, Thomas.**
(1567-1601) Born in Suffolk, Nashe studied at St. John's College, Cambridge. Pamphleteer and poet, he is perhaps best known today for *The Unfortunate Traveler* (1594), a picaresque novel.

**Nemerov, Howard.**
(1920-1991) Nemerov was born in New York. From the 1940s until his death he wrote poetry and, to a lesser degree, prose. He won a Pulitzer Prize for his *Collected Poems* (1977) and from 1988 to 1990 served as US Poet Laureate, having previously been appointed Consultant in Poetry in 1963-64.

**Olds, Sharon.**
(b. 1942) Born in San Francisco, Olds has lived in New York for many years. Her published collections include *Strike Sparks: Selected Poems* (2004); her work has appeared in numerous magazines and anthologies. Olds served as New York State Poet from 1998 to 2000 and now teaches writing workshops in New York City.

**Oliver, Mary.**
(b. 1935) Born in Maple Heights, Ohio, Oliver has spent much of her life in Massachusetts. Her first volume of poetry, *No Voyage and Other Poems*, was published in 1963. Her 1983 collection, *American Primitive*, won the Pulitzer Prize.

**Orr, Thomas Alan.**
Orr was born in Bangor, Maine. A collection of poems, *Hammers in the Fog*, appeared in 1995 from Restoration Press. Orr can be seen reading his poems in *Somewhere in Indiana* (2004), a film written and directed by Don Boner. Now living in Indiana, Orr is a rabbit farmer as well as poet.

**Paley, Grace.**
(1922-2007) Born in the Bronx, Paley spent most of her life in New York City. Known for her short stories as well as her poetry, she was a political activist, working with the War Resisters League and participating in nonviolent civil disobedience. Her titles include *The Collected Stories* (1994) *and Begin Again: Collected Poems* (2001). Paley was Poet Laureate of Vermont from 2003 until her death.

**Pastan, Linda.**
(b. 1932) Pastan, born in the Bronx, is the author of *Queen of a Rainy Country* and *The Five Stages of Grief* among other works. Pastan has said that she writes about what is around her (e.g., children, when her children were young; recently, aging friends and family). She was Poet Laureate of Maryland, where she still resides, from 1991 to 1995.

**Pereira, Peter.**
(b. 1959) Pereira is a family physician in Seattle and founder/editor of Floating Bridge Press. His first chapbook, *The Lost Twin,* appeared in 2000. A collection, *Saying the World,* followed two years later. In 2005, Pereira won the Glenna Luschei Prairie Schooner Award.

**Pollycove, Morton.**
(b. 1931) Morton Pollycove is the pen name of H. J. Van Peenen, an internist and pathologist who retired in 1990. Pollycove's output, often humorous, uncludes the poems "A Villanelle for Nitrogen Dioxide" and "A Bardic Chant for the Major Drugs", both of which appear in *The Literature* (1992).

**Reid, Christopher.**
(b. 1949) Reid, born in Hong Kong, is an illustrator as well as a poet. His titles include *Arcadia, Katerina Brac, Alphabicycle Order* (for children), and the poem *The Pub Band,* inspired by Rachel Carson's *The Silent Spring*. He is one of the founders of "Martian poetry," which uses unusual metaphors to de-familiarize day-to-day occurrences. Formerly poetry editor for Faber and Faber, Reid now teaches at the University of Hull.

**Roethke, Theodore.**
(1908-1963) Roethke published ten collections of poetry including *The Waking: Poems,* which won the Pulitzer Prize in 1954. He taught at several colleges and universities, including Michigan State University and the University of Washington. A friend of W. H. Auden, William Carlos Williams, and Stanley Kunitz, he was mentor to several well-known poets, among them David Wagoner. Roethke was born in Saginaw, Michigan.

**Rossini, Clare.**
A native of St. Paul, Minnesota, Rossini won the 1996 Akron Poetry Prize for *Winter Morning with Crow*. She teaches English and creative writing at Trinity College in Hartford, Connecticut.

**Rowe, Vernon.**
(b. 1944) Rowe is an American physician and poet whose collection *Sea Creatures and Other Poems* appeared in 1995 (Whirlybird Press).

**Samio, Maekawa.**
(1903-1990) Samio began writing tanka as a child. Born into a wealthy family, he was able to pursue writing for most of his life. He was awarded a Shaku Prize for his poetry in 1971 and was inducted into the Japan Art Academy in 1989.

**Sarton, May.**
(1912-1995) As a child, the Belgian-born Sarton fled Europe with her family to the United States. Writing into her 80's, Sarton often wrote of living alone and aging. Her voluminous body of work includes poetry, novels, journals, and two books for children. For her last two decades she lived on the coast of Maine; she died of breast cancer.

**Schorb, E. M.**
Schorb has published several collections of poetry, the latest of which, *Murderer's Day* (Purdue University Press), won the Verna Emery Poetry Prize. He lives in North Carolina.

**Sexton, Anne.**
(1928-1974) Born in Newton, Massachusetts, Sexton published her first volume of poetry in 1960. A confessional poet, much of her work deals with issues specific to women. She committed suicide in 1974. Her *Complete Poems* was published posthumously.

**Shea, John.**
Shea won the City Paper Prize in 2002 for "The Anxious Poem." His writing has appeared in magazines ranging from *The Partisan Review* to *Alfred Hitchcock's Mystery Magazine*.

**Shore, Henry.**
(1917-1977) Shore's six volumes include *The Roundabout* (1972), *The Nomad and Other Poems* (1973), and *Two Voyages* (1978). Shore, a physician, qualified in Vienna in 1936. He fled the Nazis and went to England, later working in Uganda.

**Smith, Larry.**
Smith was born in Ohio. His writings include poetry, fiction, and translations from Chinese. *A River Remains: Poems* was published in 2006. He teaches at BGSU Firelands College.

**Stafford, William.**
(1914-1993) Born in Hutchinson, Kansas, Stafford spent much of his life in Oregon, teaching at Lewis and Clark College for more than 30 years. He published more than 65 works of poetry and prose. His works have been compared to Robert Frost's. In 1970, he served as the Consultant in Poetry to the Library of Congress.

**Stallworthy, Jon.**
(b. 1935) Born in London to parents who had a year previously emigrated from New Zealand, Stallworthy is a professor of English literature at Oxford University and author of seven books of poetry, including *A Familiar Tree* (1978) and *Body Language* (2004). He edited *The Oxford Book of War Poetry* (1984).

**Stern, Gerald.**
(b. 1925) Stern was born in Pittsburgh. His thirteen collections of verse, including *Lucky Life* (1977), *This Time: New and Selected Poems* (1998), and *Everything is Burning* (2005), have earned him many awards. Stern, formerly an instructor at the University of Iowa Writer's Workshop, now lives in New Jersey.

**Stevens, Wallace.**
(1879-1955) Stevens pursued a career as a lawyer and businessman concurrently with his writing. Although his first book of poetry (*Harmonium*) was published in 1923, recognition of his status as a major poet did not come until 1954 with his *Collected Poems*. Major works include *Ideas of Order* and *The Man with the Blue Guitar*. Born in Reading, Pennsylvania, Stevens lived in Connecticut for much of his life.

**Stone, John.**
(b. 1936) Stone is an internist and cardiologist. He was professor of medicine and cardiology at Emory University School of Medicine. Among his writings are *Renaming the Streets* (1985) and *Where Water Begins: New Poems and Prose* (1998).

**Strand, Mark.**
(b. 1934) Strand was born in Prince Edward Island, Canada. He has written and edited several volumes of poetry and has published translations and three books for children. He has taught at several universities, including Columbia University and the University of Chicago. *Blizzard of One* won him the Pulitzer Prize in 1999. Strand was US Poet Laureate from 1990-1991.

**Straus, Marc J.**
An oncologist, Straus practices in New York. His poems about patients have been the source of an off-Broadway production, *Not God*. He has written nearly 100 scientific papers as well.

**Swenson, May.**
(1913-1989) Born in Logan, Utah, Swenson taught poetry at several universities and was an editor at New Directions from 1956-66. Many of her poems delight in the natural world. Others root themselves in love and eroticism, especially lesbian sexuality. Her *Love Poems*, an anthology of much of her best work, was published posthumously.

**Swir, Anna.**
(1909-1984) Swir (née Swirszczynska) was a Polish poet born in Warsaw. During the German occupation, she joined the Resistance and served as a nurse. Bearing witness to the war formed the basis of some of her writings. Her six volumes of poetry include *Building the Barricade* (1974) and *Talking to my Body* (1996).

**Takuboku, Ishikawa.**
(1886-1912) Born in Joko Temple, Japan, Takuboku was known for both tanka and free verse. His major works were two volumes of tanka poems: *A Handful of Sand* (aka "A Fistful of Sand") and *Sad Playthings* (aka "Sad Toys" or "Grieving Toys"), the latter published posthumously. He died of tuberculosis at age 27. A statue of Takuboku stands in Hakodate, Hokkaido.

**Tate, James.**
(b. 1943) Tate's *Selected Poems* won the Pulitzer Prize in 1992; *Worshipful Company of Fletchers* won the National Book Award three years later. Born in Kansas City, Missouri, Tate teaches at the University of Massachusetts, Amherst.

**Tennyson, Alfred.**
(1809-1892) Arguably the greatest Victorian poet, Tennyson was born in Somersby. Faced with financial difficulties for years, he achieved literary success with *Poems* (1842) and *In Memoriam* (1850), the latter published the same year he was appointed Poet Laureate. Tennyson was quite near-sighted and had difficulty reading and writing because of it. It is said that he composed many poems in his head.

**Thayer, William Sydney.**
(1864-1932) Born in Milton, Massachusetts, Thayer served in the U.S. Army during the First World War. A student of Sir William Osler, he went on to a long and distinguished career as a physician, researcher, and teacher at Johns Hopkins University.

**Towle, Parker.**
Towle, a neurologist, lives in New Hampshire and teaches at Dartmouth-Hitchcock Medical School. He has published three chapbooks, the latest being *Our Places*, and his poems have appeared in various anthologies. Towle has been actively involved with The Frost Place in New Hampshire.

**Van Doren, Mark.**
(1894-1972) Van Doren taught at Columbia University for over 30 years; among his students were Allen Ginsberg and Thomas Merton. He wrote poetry, novels, and criticism, and won the Pulitzer Prize in 1940 for his *Collected Poems*. Van Doren was born in Hope, Illinois.

**Vargas, Richard.**
Vargas was born in southern California and lives in New Mexico. A Mexican-American poet, his most recent collection is *American Jesus: Poems* (2007).

**Wagoner, David.**
(b. 1926) Wagoner, born in Massillon, Ohio, lives in Washington. Author of nearly 20 poetry collections, Wagoner has received numerous awards for his poetry. Titles include *Good Morning and Good Night* (2005), *Walt Whitman Bathing* (1996), and *Who Shall Be the Sun?* (1978), based on the folklore and tales of indigenous peoples of the Northwest coast and plateau regions. Francis Ford Coppola adapted one of Wagoner's ten novels, *The Escape Artist* (1965), for the screen.

**Wei, Wang.**
(699-761) Wang Wei was a Chinese physician, poet, musician, and painter who lived during the Tang Dynasty and whose landscape paintings were influential in later eras. Following his wife's death, he lived a monastic life for the next 30 years, and his art is said to reflect his melancholy feelings.

**White, Kelley Jean.**
White is a poet and pediatrician in Philadelphia. Her poetry collections are *The Patient Presents* and *Late*, as well as a chapbook, *Against Medical Advice*.

**Wilbur, Richard.**
(b. 1921) Wilbur was born in New York City. He won the Pulitzer Prize in 1957 for *Things of This World* and again in 1989 for *New and Collected Poems*. Wilbur was the second official US Poet Laureate (1987-88). Also acclaimed for his translations of 17th century French drama, Wilbur has taught at Harvard, Wesleyan University, and Smith College.

**Williams, C. K.**
(b. 1936) Williams was born in Newark, New Jersey. He has written numerous books of poetry and translations and has been the recipient of many awards, including the Pulitzer Prize for his collection *Repairs.* Other titles include *The Singing, Flesh and Blood,* and *The Vigil.* Williams teaches in the Writing Program at Princeton University.

**Williams, Miller.**
(b. 1930) Born in Hoxie, Arkansas, Miller Williams has published 26 books. He read a commemorative poem at President Clinton's second inauguration (1997), becoming the third poet to have been selected to read at a President's inauguration.

**Williams, William Carlos.**
(1883-1963) One of the best-known American poets of the 20th century, William Carlos Williams was a pediatrician who practiced in Rutherford, New Jersey, his birthplace. In 1963, he won the Pulitzer Prize for *Pictures from Breughel.* Williams also wrote plays, essays, autobiography, and a novel.

**Woods, Christopher J.**
Woods is an English doctor and poet. A collection of poems, *Recovery*, appeared in 1993.

**Wordsworth, William.**
(1770-1850) Wordsworth is one of the major figures of Romanticism, and his *Lyrical Ballads* (1798), published jointly with Samuel Taylor Coleridge, stands as one of the great landmarks of English literature. Queen Victoria appointed Wordsworth Poet Laureate in 1843. His long poem, "The Prelude," never finally revised to Wordsworth's liking, was published posthumously.

**Wright, John.**
(b. 1930) After retiring from medicine, Wright concentrated on poetry. Unlike some physician/poets, he draws much of his inspiration from nature. *As Though Praying: Poems from Decatur Island* was published by Bluestone Books in 2002. An earlier collection is *Through an Old Wooden Bowl* (1999). Wright's poems have appeared in a variety of journals and magazines.

**Yeats, W. B.**
(1865-1939) William Butler Yeats was one of the foremost literary figures of the 20th century. Ireland's greatest lyric poet, the Dublin-born Yeats won the Nobel Prize for Literature in 1923. He led the Irish Literary Revival and was also politically active. A founder of the Irish National Theatre Company, he wrote many short plays.

**Young, David.**
(b. 1936) Young, author of ten books of verse, has also translated many poems, including those of Miroslav Holub. He is one of the founders and editors of the magazine *Field*, published by Oberlin Press. His poems are found in numerous anthologies and have garnered many awards. He teaches English at Oberlin College.

**Young, George.**
(b. 1938) Young is a Fellow of the American College of Physicians. "Tell Me" first appeared in *Annals of Internal Medicine.*

**Zinsser, Hans.**
(1878-1940) Zinsser, a physician/bacteriologist, was born in New York City. He worked for Harvard Medical School for nearly two decades and is known for his important work on the typhus vaccine.

# Permissions

Agodon, Kelli Russell: "Snapshot of a Lump" from *Small Knots* © 2004 by Kelli Agodon. Cherry Grove Collections. Reprinted by permission of the author.

Akiko, Yosano: "agonizing beyond words" from *Modern Japanese Tanka: An Anthology*, translated by Makoto Ueda, © 1996 by Columbia University Press. Reprinted by permission of the publisher.

Angelou, Maya: "Old Folks Laugh" from *I Shall Not Be Moved* © 1990 by Maya Angelou. Used by permission of Random House, Inc. and the Helen Brann Agency, Inc.

Appleman, Philip: "Birthday Card to My Mother" from *New and Selected Poems, 1956-1996* © 1996 by Philip Appleman. Reprinted by permission of the University of Arkansas Press, www.uapress.com.

Auden, W. H.: "Funeral Blues" from *Collected Poems* and *Another Time* © 1976 by The Executors of The Estate of W. H. Auden. Used by permission of Random House Inc. and Faber and Faber Ltd.

Barnstone, Willis: "At My Funeral" from *Life Watch* © 2003 by Willis Barnstone. Reprinted by permission of BOA Editions, Ltd.

Bascom, George: "Meeting on Quality Assurance," "Anatomy," "Destiny," and "Massive Trauma" from *Faint Echoes* © 1991 by George Bascom; "Departmental Function" from *Medicine Circles* © 1993 by George Bascom. Reprinted by permission of The Family of George Bascom.

Bashō: "Sick on a Journey" from *On Love and Barley: Haiku of Bashō*. Translated with an introduction by Lucien Stryk (Penguin Classics, 1985) © 1985 by Lucien Stryk. Reprinted by permission of University of Hawaii Press and Penguin Group (UK).

Beaumont, Jeanne Marie: "Afraid So" from *Curious Conduct* © 2004 by Jeanne Marie Beaumont. Reprinted by permission of BOA Editions, Ltd., www.boaeditions.org.

Berlin, Richard: "Open You Up," first published in *How JFK Killed My Father*, Pearl Editions © 2004. Winner, Pearl Poetry Prize 2002. Please visit www.richardmberlin.com.

Berry, Wendell: "The Mad Farmer Liberation Front" from *The Collected Poems of Wendell Berry, 1957-1982*, © 1985 by Wendell Berry; published by North Point Press, Berkeley, California. Reprinted by permission of the author.

Bly, Robert: "Gratitude to Old Teachers" from *Meditations on the Insatiable Soul* © 1994 by Robert Bly. Reprinted by permission of HarperCollins Publishers.

Booth, Philip: "A Man in Maine" from *Relations: New and Selected Poems* © 1986 by Philip Booth. Used by permission of Viking Penguin, a division of Penguin Group (USA) Inc.

Bosch, Daniel: "Tree of Knowledge" from *Bostonia*, Spring 2000. "HMO" from *Slate*, 13 July 2004. Reprinted by permission of the author.

Jones, Alice: "Communal Living" from *Blood and Bone: Poems by Physicians,* Angela Belli and Jack Coulehan, eds., © 1998 University of Iowa Press. Reprinted by permission of the author. "Prayer" from *The Knot* © 1992 by Alice Jones. Published by Alice James Books. Reprinted by permission of the author.

Kelly-DeWitt, Susan: "Bypass" appears in *The Fortunate Islands* © 2008 Marick Press, and also in *Susan Kelly-DeWitt: Greatest Hits* © 2003 Pudding House Publications. Reprinted by the permission of Susan Kelly-DeWitt.

Kenyon, Jane: "Having It Out With Melancholy" from *Constance* © 1993 The Estate of Jane Kenyon. Reprinted by the permission of Graywolf Press, Saint Paul, Minnesota. "The Sick Wife" from *Otherwise: New & Selected Poems* © 1997 The Estate of Jane Kenyon. Reprinted by permission of Graywolf Press.

Koch, Kenneth: "To Stammering" from *Collected Poems of Kenneth Koch* © 2005 by The Kenneth Koch Literary Estate. Used by permission of Alfred A. Knopf, a division of Random House, Inc.

Koertge, Ron: "With a Million Things to Do, the Doctor Muses, Anyway" from *Making Love to Roget's Wife: Poems New and Selected* © 1997 by Ron Koertge. Reprinted by permission of University of Arkansas Press. "The Doctor Sighs" from *Geography of the Forehead* © 2000 by Ron Koertge. Reprinted by permission of University of Arkansas Press, www.uapress.com.

Kooser, Ted: "My Grandfather Dying" and "After the Funeral: Cleaning Out the Medicine Cabinet" from *Flying at Night: Poems 1965 – 1985* © 2005. "The Urine Specimen" from *One World at a Time* © 1985. Reprinted by permission of University of Pittsburgh Press. "A Spiral Notebook" from *Delights & Shadows* © 2004 by Ted Kooser. Reprinted by permission of Copper Canyon Press, www.coppercanyonpress.org.

Larkin, Philip: "Hospital Visits" and "Skin" from *Philip Larkin: Collected Poems* © 1988. Reprinted by permission of Faber and Faber Ltd and The Marvell Press.

Lowry, Malcolm: "Homeopathic Blues in J" from *The Collected Poetry of Malcolm Lowry* © 1982 by The Estate of Malcolm Lowry. Reprinted by permission of SLL/Sterling Lord Literistic, Inc.

Lurie, Bobbi: "The Psychiatrist Says She's Severely Demented" from *Letter from the Lawn* © 2006. Reprinted by permission of WordTech Communications.

Lux, Thomas: "The Swimming Pool" from *Half-Promised Land* © 1986 by Thomas Lux. "Impingement Syndrome" from *New and Selected Poems, 1975-1995* © 1997 by Thomas Lux. Reprinted by permission of Houghton Mifflin Company. All rights reserved.

Mahon, Derek: "Everything is Going to Be All Right" from *Collected Poems* © 1999. Reprinted by kind permission of the author and The Gallery Press, Loughcrew, Oldcastle, County Meath, Ireland.

Mehta, Diane: "1 in 300" from *Prairie Schooner*, volume 79, number 2 (Summer 2005). © 2005 by University of Nebraska Press. Reprinted by permission of University of Nebraska Press.

Merton, Thomas: "The Woodcarver" from *The Way of Chuang Tzu* © 1965 by The Abbey of Gethsemani. Reprinted by permission of New Directions Publishing Corp.

Wilbur, Richard P.: "To an American Poet Just Dead" from *Ceremony and Other Poems* © 1950, © renewed 1978 by Richard Wilbur. Reprinted by permission of Harcourt, Inc.

Williams, C. K.: "The Dance" and "Dissections" from *Collected Poems* © 2006 by C. K. Williams. Reprinted by permission of Farrar, Straus and Giroux.

Williams, Miller: "Going Deaf" and "At the Children's Hospital in Little Rock" from *Points of Departure: Poems by Miller Williams* © 1995 by Miller Williams. Reprinted by permission of the poet and University of Illinois Press.

Williams, William Carlos: "The Last Words of My English Grandmother" from *Collected Poems: 1909-1939, Volume 1* © 1938 by New Directions Publishing Corp. Reprinted by permission of New Directions Publishing Corp.

Yeats, W. B.: "When You Are Old" and "A Friend's Illness." Reprinted by permission of A P Watt Ltd.

Zinsser, Hans: "Now is Death merciful…" to "Serene and proud as when you loved me best." from *Spring, Summer & Autumn* ©1942 by Alfred A. Knopf, © renewed 1969 by Ruby Handforth Zinsser. Used by permission of Alfred A. Knopf, a division of Random House, Inc.